A Woman
Who Trusts
God

## Books by Debbie Alsdorf

*Deeper: Living in the Reality of God's Love*
*A Different Kind of Wild: Is Your Faith Too Tame?*
*The Faith Dare: 30 Days to Live Your Life to the Fullest*

# A Woman Who Trusts God

Finding the Peace
You Long For

Debbie Alsdorf

Revell
a division of Baker Publishing Group
Grand Rapids, Michigan

© 2011 by Debbie Alsdorf

Published by Revell
a division of Baker Publishing Group
P.O. Box 6287, Grand Rapids, MI 49516-6287
www.revellbooks.com

Printed in the United States of America

Library of Congress Cataloging-in-Publication Data
Alsdorf, Debbie.
    A woman who trusts God : finding the peace you long for / Debbie Alsdorf.
      p.  cm.
    Includes bibliographical references.
    ISBN 978-0-8007-3368-1 (pbk.)
    1. Christian women—Religious life. I. Title.
  BV4527.A465 2011
  248.8′43—dc23                                 2011024805

12   13   14   15   16   17       7   6   5   4   3   2

Dedicated with love to my friend
Bettina Belter

Painted calla lilies will forever remind me that
God can triumph over any present problem! I
love you and how you choose to trust God in all
the frustrating meantime places of life.

You will keep in perfect peace
    all who trust in you,
    all whose thoughts are fixed on you!
Trust in the LORD always,
    for the LORD GOD is the eternal Rock.
Isaiah 26:3–4 NLT

Depend on GOD and keep at it
    because in the Lord God you have a sure thing.
Isaiah 26:4 Message

# Contents

# Acknowledgments

Relationships are the gift of life. I would like to thank the people who have inspired, encouraged, and prayed for me while in the process of this book, especially Ali Contois, Patty Hanway, Patty Rose, Voni Ribera, and Sharon Randall.

Voni Ribera, thank you for giving me your father's book on Philippians. A special thanks to Avon Malone for his hard work—he is with the Lord but is still touching lives here on earth. Thank you, Avon, for your work for God's kingdom.

The Grooveys and the Groovettes! You know who you are! Simply awesome and radically fun! To use an old-school phrase—you light up my life! Thanks.

Christy Harper, Val Rousch, Lori Sisemore, Lorri Steer—thanks for being modern-day encouragers. Priceless!

Nicku Bastani—thanks for lending me your Mac when my computer wasn't working. Terry Perazza—thanks for being an extraordinary neighbor and friend who is always ready to help out. Liana Tate—your coffee dates and friendship are special gifts. Thanks for both. Just being with you helps me trust God more.

Britta Usedom—watching your process has increased my trust in a God who is always at work in human lives. You are very special.

My precious family—Ray, Justin, Janae, Ashley, Austin, Cameron, and Megan. You are all a joy in my life. You encourage me, give me space when I am writing, have coffee with me when I am processing, and love me through all of life's meantimes. Giant hugs!

This book was written while planning two weddings, so I want to mention Janae Brier, my new daughter-in-love, and Austin Jones, my new son-in-love. While I lived through the singleness of my adult children, I didn't know that God had the two of you planned to step in and be part of our family. Your entrance into our lives is my daily reminder that we can trust God—all the time.

Wrapping up my thanks, I must mention my editor Vicki Crumpton. Thanks for all you have meant to me as a writer. You polish off the rough spots so women can be ministered to by the words in my books. And thanks to all those at Baker Publishing Group who have worked on my books. I am blessed by the privilege of being a Revell author. My literary agent, Les Stobbe—thank you for believing in me and the things God has called me to do.

I saved the best for last. All thanks goes to Jesus Christ, who has redeemed me, continually pulling me up out of my own ways and into his arms. I love him the most, thank him the most, and pray that he will be pleased and honored as women learn to place their trust in him alone.

# Introduction

## *Heart to Heart*

Can I start this book with a disclaimer? Some days I am not a woman who trusts God with all my cares, problems, and details. There, I said it. Truth is, there are times I sit and stew in a self-pity party of insecurity, worry, and fear. And, yes, there are times I try to overanalyze and figure out everything on my own, seeking for a piece of control. But I have found that when I don't trust God with my life and my circumstances, I have very little peace. I have experienced both—trust and fear. And I like trust and the life it gives me much more than I like the anxiety that comes from relying on my own limited resources.

I want to grow as a woman who trusts God—especially in the ordinary things. So I am hoping that you will walk with me through the pages of this book and through the challenges we both face in life. One thing is certain: God longs to give us his peace just as much as we long to receive it. And there is no joy in this world like a mind at peace—it trumps everything.

I don't know where you live or what your situation is, but I do know that even if our lives are different, we have much in common. You and I go through tough stuff in this life. From daily frustrations and responsibilities to the bigger challenges, life is hard, and if we are not careful, the hard things can overwhelm us and rob us of joy while diluting our faith.

I am quite an expert on living in freak-out mode, so I speak from experience. But a few years ago it dawned on me that there really is a better way to live and that I no longer had to be bound by the way I had done things in the past. I could learn a healthier and more spiritually alive way to approach life. I didn't have to go from A to Z in one giant step. I could go from A to B, then travel along to C, going through the steps of growth while each and every situation played out in my life. In his Word, God teaches us the basic principles for living this way, and I have great news for you. These principles work!

This year I have walked alongside women who have gone through things that are unthinkably difficult to endure: the death of a child, the death of a spouse, financial collapse, marital unfaithfulness, addictions of every kind—alcohol, food, drug— and the loss of their dreams as life collapsed around them. Times have been hard.

I have also walked alongside women who have endured garden-variety trials: nothing earth-shattering, but difficult situations that drained their joy, things like unreasonable husbands, unruly children, unmanageable friendships, and frustration with a life that is not the fairy tale they hoped it would be.

And, finally, I am aware of many women who are just fine. Thank God! They are walking along, trying to grow, weathering life's seasons, and staying above water. These women don't think they have it all together; they just keep praying for the grace to stay the course.

So like I said, we have much in common. All of us, no matter where we are today, have a life to be lived. None of us gets to choose how or when we will die, but each of us gets to choose the direction in which we will live. And our direction determines our destination. I often wonder if we realize that the choices we make determine how much peace we experience. I am not talking about big choices as much as little ones—the tiny daily steps of trust. That is what this book is about. Our journey together is one of looking at our choices—of attitude, belief, and mind-set.

I wish we could sit down over a cup of coffee and talk through the difficult spots in life. We could encourage one another, commit to praying for one another, and part ways a little better because of the sincere exchange of real-life stuff. If we could spend some time together, I would want to open the book of Philippians—a letter written by the apostle Paul to the early church. He gives such amazing insight, and I know we would be mutually challenged and encouraged. But since I can't meet you at the local coffee shop, these pages will have to do for now.

It is my prayer that as we journey together through the spiritual direction that is found in Philippians, we will gain new courage to trust that all of life—even the pain and suffering—is part and parcel of the reality of the human condition here on earth. In no way do I have it all figured out, so we will just walk side by side, heart to heart, woman to woman, gaining strength during our difficult "meantime" places—those places in between where we wait for God to answer our prayers, solve our problems, or make some sense of it all. One thing is certain: real life requires something bigger than ourselves.

These pages are for women living in the meantime:

- those who want to live well while waiting for a solution to be realized

- those who hear the word *trust* and cringe because they don't know how to trust a God they cannot see while living in circumstances that are difficult and disappointing
- those who hear the word *peace* and dismiss it because they are living with no peace at all and don't know how to find it
- those who want to live the life God has called them to and find joy in it, no matter what current circumstances they are facing or what tomorrow might bring
- those who want to learn how to walk in truth, living in the promises of God rather than just talking about them
- those who are tired of living lives limited by self—habits, weaknesses, ruts, attitudes, and other things they can't seem to break free from
- those who want to be changed, transformed, and conformed into the image of God—and want to know how it happens

If there was never rain, there would not be flowers in the garden of your life. Rain, though soggy and annoying, is a beautiful expression of God's provision. The harsh times in life are the same—though difficult and discouraging, they will prove to be the change agent we need, making us beautiful women who have learned to trust God with everything. Trust doesn't happen overnight; it happens step-by-step, lesson by lesson—in the furnace of the meantime.

My favorite devotional of all time is Oswald Chambers's *My Utmost for His Highest*. This particular section is something I carry with me as I learn to trust God. Read it, think about it, and maybe you too will be changed by its message. The main thing that is necessary as we learn to trust is the surrender of our thoughts and attitudes to the truth of God's faithfulness. As you begin this book, consider the words penned by Oswald Chambers years ago:

Is your mind stayed on God or is it starved? Starvation of the mind, caused by neglect, is one of the chief sources of exhaustion and weakness in a servant's life. If you have never used your mind to place yourself before God, begin to do it now. There is no reason to wait for God to come to you. You must turn your thoughts and your eyes away from the face of idols and look to Him and be saved.

Your mind is the greatest gift God has given you and it ought to be devoted entirely to Him. You should seek to be "bringing every thought into captivity to the obedience of Christ . . ." (2 Cor. 10:5) This will be one of the greatest assets of your faith when a time of trial comes, because then your faith and the Spirit of God will work together. . . . Your mind will no longer be at the mercy of your impulsive thinking but will always be used in service to God.[1]

This book will give you a little to think about each day as you consider where you are and what you are going through. Underline and highlight, answer the journaling questions, and if you are really brave, do this with a friend. In the back of the book you will find a five-week study guide. I added this for those who want to dig deeper into Philippians by themselves or with a group.

Here's to the meantime! May we learn to live well, laugh out loud in the face of our problems, and grow through the hard stuff! God himself is forming something beautiful within us.

# 1

## The Meantime

*What It Is and Why You Need a Plan for It*

I thank my God every time I remember you . . . being confident of this, that he who began a good work in you will carry it on to completion until the day of Christ Jesus.

Philippians 1:3, 6

It was a great afternoon sharing the gift of friendship. We ate our favorite salads, drank our favorite spiced ice tea, and caught up on months of each other's lives. But as soon as we walked out of the restaurant, we were once again thrust into our real worlds, facing small daily annoyances and bigger real-life problems. As we said good-bye, my friend smiled. "I know things will get better, *but in the meantime*, I have a lot to face—chemo, radiation, and finding a wig."

We both laughed at her finally becoming a blonde—through a Dolly Parton wig. But there was nothing funny about her immediate path in life. Recently diagnosed with cancer, she was on the road to recovery, but in the meantime, life was going to take some very difficult twists and turns.

In the meantime . . .

We all know about the meantime. It is that place in between a problem recognized and a solution realized. It is the dash between point A and point B. The meantime is a part of life. Whether it be getting through the day or getting through the next few months or the next few years, the meantime is all around us. This place in life doesn't have to revolve around big things. The meantime is even in the little situations we face each day and throughout each week.

Just today I had a meantime experience. I was driving through town, singing to the radio and enjoying my morning. Then my cell phone rang. A frantic call from someone in my family sent my mind spinning and my heart racing. I immediately thought, *God, please come through and help us in this situation!* I knew he would, but I didn't know God's timing or how long the problem would take to resolve.

As my anxiety level rose a bit, I had a choice to make. The situation was real and brought immediate concern, but God was bigger than the situation. Knowing the truth—that God was bigger—how would I live, in the meantime? In other words, how would I live while I was waiting for the situation to be resolved? Would I trust God while waiting for answers to the problem at hand? Or would I freak out and temporarily forget there is a God who claims to be bound to faithfulness toward me?

It's not a question of *if* but a question of how will we live *when* life presents a problem, a disappointment, devastation, a loss, or a daily annoyance. How will we live in that space between our prayer to God and the answer on earth? Does the meantime rob us of joy? Does it steal our peace and dilute our faith? Does it distract our focus? Does the meantime open the door for chaos and worry?

Certainly, as life unfolds, it has the potential to shake us up and dilute our faith. I can fall prey to that temptation while trying to figure out my problems or trying to fix my life. Truth is, when I am in a meantime place, I often excuse my behavior because I am upset. I suppose that because most people live this way, I have not stopped to realize that God wants so much more for me than living from freak-out to freak-out. I like the idea of living from peace to peace or from glory to glory as I am being conformed into his image one moment at a time.

## Sitting in Philippians

A few years back I began sitting in Philippians—a letter the apostle Paul wrote to the church in Philippi. What do I mean by "sitting" in Philippians? Simply put, I read the book over and over, lingering in parts that jumped out at me, spending time with truths that seemed challenging or impractical, looking for themes and key points, then digesting them for practical application. As I prayed over the text, I asked God to teach me, to infuse the truths of Scripture into my heart and mind. I asked to be changed by truth and for the grace and strength to walk it out in my life. Sitting in a book of the Bible, or a chapter in the Bible, can be a quick sit of a week or a much longer stay. I have sat in certain passages for up to a year.

As I sat with the spiritual direction in the letter the apostle Paul wrote thousands of years ago, I began to realize that life can unravel people or bring them to a continual place of greater peace. I began paying attention, because I had already mastered the steps to coming undone and unraveled. What I needed to learn was something new—how to walk in peace, contentment, and victory. Maybe you could use some encouragement in these areas too.

Though there are many experts on the human condition, no expert can match the knowledge that God has of our condition.

He made us, he sustains us, and whether we realize it or not, he has provided a way for us to live our lives. But because he is not a celebrity or on the talk show circuit, we discount what he has to offer and replace it with the latest craze or the newest techniques marketed to us by the world's experts. This creates a problem, because the meantime for Christians is much more than a circumstance to walk through; it is a life span between our real home and the one we live in now—the space between earth's realities and heaven's promise.

## From Here to Eternity

We are told throughout the Bible that as believers in Jesus Christ this world is not our home. Yet, since this is all we know for now, we live like this is all there is. In doing so, we live our lives based on human philosophy, self strength, and fleeting feelings. When things don't go our way, we fall prey to discouragement and defeat. Some day we will be with Jesus, but in the meantime, we are living in this world with people who rub us the wrong way, disappoint us, hurt us, and cause us a lot of pain. In this life, we have bills to pay, children to raise, problems to solve. Add to that list aging and illness and securing our future. There is a lot to think about, in the meantime. And let's not forget the smaller problems that cause each and every day to be some type of meantime place.

Take work for instance. You wake up, want to stay home, but know the responsible thing to do is to show up for work. So off to work you go, looking forward to the end of the day. In the meantime, you have eight to ten hours to live your life. That's a lot of meantime hours. Will they be wasted in mindless waiting? Or will they be lived fully even though you are eager to be somewhere else?

Though Jesus Christ does not have a TV talk show, the Holy Bible is a best seller and has been for years. The Bible lays out truths and life applications for us so that we can know how to live in this life—while preparing ourselves for the one to come. Trouble is we don't pay enough attention to what has been laid out for us. We read the Bible, create spiritual theories about it, but fail to walk it out day after day in the meantime places of our real worlds.

I have read Philippians many times over the years. I have memorized the key passages. But as I began sitting with the simple truths again, I was amazed at how practical all of Philippians is in regard to this place called the meantime.

As I sat, prayed, and thought about Paul and the writing of this letter, the thing that continually jumped out at me was that he was not in a "good" place when he wrote it, but he lived in a "good" place despite his actual circumstances. Think of it—the apostle Paul wrote this letter to the church in Philippi while in prison. He was certainly in a meantime lockdown! He had no control over his circumstances and could not free himself from jail. But there were a few things he did have control over:

- the attitude with which he faced his circumstances
- the direction he then took each day and each step
- where he put his hope and trust each day

Likewise, we face circumstances over which we have little control. We cannot control other people's choices, even though their choices do affect us. We cannot control certain things like disease and disaster, though both are a part of our world.

What we do have control over are the three things Paul had control over: attitude, direction, and trust. In other words, what we have control over is what we set our minds on.

> Since, then, you have been raised with Christ, set your hearts on things above, where Christ is, seated at the right hand of God. Set your mind on things above, not on earthly things.
>
> Colossians 3:1–2

21

Paul was clearly focused on God's purpose in all things. He begins his letter by thanking God with prayer and joy for his friends as he reminds them that God will complete his own good work in them (Phil. 1:6). This was his stand, his focus, and the way he lived: to give others courage by helping them believe the truth that God is always at work.

## Interval Training

In the meantime, will we set our mind on the problem and how long it's taking for a resolution? Or will we set our mind on the truths that in the meantime God is with us, is working in all the hard stuff, is teaching us something because of it, and always has our back?

*Webster's Dictionary* defines the meantime as "the period between occurrences: an interval." Perhaps what we need is interval training! And that is exactly what Paul holds out to us in Philippians—interval training for living in this life while we wait for the next.

It would be ridiculous to think we could wave a wand or sprinkle some spiritual fairy dust and get a quick fix for our real-life problems. But we shouldn't be too quick to dismiss the basic steps and principles we find in God's Word. Think how our lives would be different if we paid attention to them and set our hearts toward living them out in our lives. The spiritual practice of walking in biblical truth is often called a discipline of the believer's life. This discipline can help lead us into a mind-set of trust and an inner atmosphere of true peace.

This book is a call to live the life God has called us to. God has given us life and shown us how to live. It's time to get serious about life, redefining it, reclaiming it for God's purposes and plans. One thing is certain: he has plans for you, plans that are good. Those plans cannot take place if you are living your life on your terms. It's time for us all to come back to him in every area—surrendering, once again, our lives into the arms and care of the God who gave us our first breath and will be with us to our last.

I have been through enough to know that the meantime is often mean. And I continue to learn how to get outside the box of "me" in order to deal with what is happening around me or to me. I am hoping this book will be a journey through the principles in Philippians that will change us and shape how we live. For this change to take place, we will have to practice remembering the truth of who God is and how faithful he is to his people.

## Why Remembering Is Important

I don't know about you, but my good attitude can change the moment my circumstances change. I forget the things I need to remember. It's like I have sudden amnesia concerning God and his faithfulness. And when I forget, I tend to spiral into a place of worry, fear, and hopelessness. In that place, I easily begin to depend on myself rather than turn to God and his grace. Perhaps like me you easily fall prey to the enemy's strategy of getting us to focus on anything other than God when times are hard.

This is a book of remembrance, a tool to help you remember the presence of Christ in the middle of the difficult places in your life. I have the hardest time in the middle of a problem, probably because I want to control the outcome and realize I can't. Though this book will not change your problem, it can help you look up and change your perspective. It is my prayer that each page will give you a little hope for the journey.

Our problems aren't resolved overnight, and we all need the most help while in the middle of a problem. So I wrote this book in short chapters for you to chew on, processing your personal meantime and finding God and help through his Word. You can read it straight through. You can turn to a topic that seems to fit a particular need on a particular day. Whatever way you read it, it is my prayer that you will remember that God loves you, he provides for your every need, and he has predestined you to be conformed into his image—and that happens in the rough spots of life. Finally, I know God wants each of us to remember that nothing can separate us from the love of God that is in Christ Jesus our Lord. And that translates into *no thing*!

> Who shall separate us from the love of Christ? Shall trouble, or hardship or persecution or famine or nakedness or danger or sword? . . . No, in all these things we are more than conquerors through him who loved us. For I am convinced that neither death nor life, neither angels nor demons, neither the present nor the future, nor any powers, neither height nor depth, nor anything else in all creation, will be able to separate us from the love of God that is in Christ Jesus our Lord.
>
> Romans 8:35, 37–39

Today is the day. As we take this journey through Philippians, we will discover ways to navigate life in the good times, the bad times, and all the spaces in between.

Each chapter ends by asking you to reflect on your thoughts and listen to God whispering to you. The journaling is followed by a short prayer. These prayers are meant to help you start to talk to the Lord about your situation. If they help you, great. If you are comfortable praying and don't need them, that is fine too. The important thing is learning to trust God in the meantimes of life. Here is an example.

**In my meantime place, I am learning . . .**

That I typically get all freaked out when things do not go as planned. In those times, the last thing I am thinking of is praying for help from God or rejoicing that I am his. I am reacting to my circumstances rather than reacting to the truth and promises in God's Word.

**In my meantime place, God is requiring me to . . .**

Pay attention to my attitude and actions when things are not optimal. I need to make prayer a first line of defense against going down emotionally and mentally. I also need to realize that difficult times are a part of life and quit expecting they will not happen. I need to learn to look to God and trust him when they do. Counting to ten when emotions hit helps too.

### Prayer

*Lord, it is so easy to focus on my problem rather than on your power. Give me the grace to live above my problems with the view of your faithfulness covering me in each of life's situations. In the practical, guide me. In the spiritual, train me. In the places in between, steady me for the duration of the problem at hand. I surrender all that overwhelms me today into your hands. Amen.*

# 2

## Problems Are Inevitable

### *Living Overwhelmed Is Optional*

And this is my prayer: that your love may abound more and more in knowledge and depth of insight, so that you may be able to discern what is best and may be pure and blameless for the day of Christ, filled with the fruit of righteousness that comes through Jesus Christ—to the glory and praise of God.

Philippians 1:9–11

Life has a way of surprising us. Sometimes the surprises are good—like an unexpected gift or the perfect pair of jeans. But not all surprises are good. Some surprises take our breath away, bully our faith away, and leave us worn-out. It was Paul's prayer that his friends would be able to discern what is best, and if he could be with us today, that would be his prayer for us too. He would coach us in the ways of truth. He would help us understand that life is hard and that God is always good. He would lift up our chins, pray for us, and undoubtedly preach to us from what he knew to be true about Christ's workings in human lives. One thing is certain: the meantime usually starts with a sudden unexpected turn of events and can be difficult to handle. Another thing is certain: the meantimes in life can change us if we yield to God in the midst of them.

### Expect the Unexpected

It was a great Monday morning. I woke up with boundless energy, had a meaningful morning conversation with my husband, and looked forward to the plans for the rest of the day. As my husband left for work, I stood at the kitchen door cheerfully waving good-bye. But something dampened our otherwise perfect morning, literally.

While walking out through the garage, my husband stopped, looked puzzled, and wiped his brow. A drop of water. Another drop, a third drop, and it became obvious that water was dripping from our garage ceiling. A quick look and we realized the water had to be coming from our son's room directly above the garage. While my husband waited downstairs, I ran as quickly as I could up to my son's room to make sure everything was okay.

But things were not okay. As I walked into the room, my feet sank into a carpet resembling wet grass. I knew we had a problem, and a big one at that. I began screaming for my husband, startling my son and waking up the entire house. We wondered if a pipe had burst in the night or if the toilet in his adjoining bathroom had overflowed. One thing was for sure. Without any advance warning, our lives were turned upside down in a moment. We were hurled into the meantime—a space of time that caused upheaval in our home for about seven weeks!

What started out as a fine day ended with furniture in our hallways, our son living out of boxes and sleeping downstairs, and contractors and repairmen in and out of our house—a few hours here, a few hours there—all the way up to the Christmas holidays.

Having the disaster happen right before the holiday season only added to the stress of the situation.

- It was not good timing—the meantime never is.
- It was inconvenient—the meantime always is.
- It was exhausting to live differently—the meantime takes you out of your comfort zone.

Despite the frustration, I was determined to learn how to live in the challenging space in between the onset of trouble or crisis—my house in complete chaos—and the resolving of the problem—my house being put back together again. By the looks of things, it was not going to be a quick or inexpensive fix.

## When Bad Things Happen, God Is Still in Control

Truth be told, my normal way of handling an interruption like this would not be pretty. I would be stressed, overwhelmed, and negative until the problem could be taken care of. I remember years ago when a counselor pointed out a pattern in my life. When a problem arose, I began stressing, spinning, worrying, and, yes, obsessing over what to do. You probably are calm, collected, and don't relate to my approach, but just in case you do, I have since found that there is a better way to live.

Faced with a major catastrophe taking over my house, something within me knew that God really could give me a new kind of peace and victory over my situation. Times like these are part of life, and I wanted to learn how to trust God when it seemed easier to moan and complain.

I had just started teaching the book of Philippians to the women at our local church. We called the study Living the Life, and now, through trial and error, I was about to embark on my own journey of learning what it means to live the life God has planned for me when life isn't much fun. Facing a problem with that faith-centered attitude requires a firm belief that every problem can be a positive growth experience. In other words, something good can come out of something not so good. I was about to embark on the challenge of remembering that when bad things happen, God is still in control and is still with me. Quite frankly, this basic biblical truth can evaporate from our memory when life is difficult. It's tempting to think God has forgotten you when things aren't going well.

It's easy to think the stories of the Bible are outdated and don't relate to our modern lives. We don't eat manna or see water turned to wine. We don't see burning bushes or parted seas. But every story in the Bible declares to us who God is and how he works in human lives. We see personal intervention and plenty of meantimes in the pages of Scripture. And just look at what Scripture says about all those stories:

> For everything that was written in the past was written to teach us, so that through endurance and the encouragement of the Scriptures we might have hope.
>
> Romans 15:4

If there were a "like" button on my Bible, I would definitely put "like" by this verse! The stories are there to teach us, and in learning, we will gain endurance and hope.

The reality is, many times in life you and I will face difficult times. During those times, we can get confused about God and his care for us. We start asking a lot of whys. Why does God allow bad things to happen? Why is there so much evil? Why can't he just give me a break? If he loves me, then why am I suffering?

I think Paul was teaching a groundbreaking principle when he said, "For it has been granted to you on behalf of Christ not only to believe on him, but also to suffer for him" (Phil. 1:29). And though I am not sure I like *that* verse, I have to acknowledge that it is there to teach me and guide me in the storms.

Randy Alcorn addresses the questions of suffering and evil in his book *If God Is Good*. He says, "We live between Genesis 3 and Revelation 20, between Eden and the New Earth. Things are *not* all right with the world."[1] And the reason things are not all right is because in Genesis 3 sin entered and everything changed. Now we wait for the new earth, the place God has prepared and promised to those who believe. But in the meantime, we need hope to face all the things here and now, for today we are living in that place in between, right smack dab in the middle of the meantime places of life.

Scripture helps us to put our troubles into proper perspective, and it's wonderful that Jesus Christ himself gave us a heads-up about real life.

> I have told you these things, so that in Me you may have [perfect] peace and confidence. In the world you have tribulation and trials and distress and frustration; but be of good cheer [take courage; be confident, certain, undaunted]! For I have overcome the world. [I have deprived it of power to harm you and have conquered it for you.]
>
> John 16:33 AMP

Right now I am thinking of that saying "Mama said there'd be days like this," and I am reminded that Jesus said there'd be days like this. But he also said these days could be lived with cheer and confidence because he has deprived them of the power to harm us or conquer us. Wow! Now that is a different way to look at things when they go wrong, isn't it? That leads us straight into the key principle for how to live in the meantime:

if God is with us in the hard times, then being overwhelmed is optional rather than a mandatory lifestyle.

## Living Overwhelmed Is a Choice

Our God is a "green" God. He recycles everything in our life to further our growth and increase our faith in him. No matter what the situation is, surrender it to the Lord. Ask him to work out the details, lead you through the particulars, and give you the grace and strength not just to go through the annoyances but to grow through them.

> Trust in the LORD with all your heart
> and lean not on your own understanding;
> in all your ways submit to him,
> and he will make your paths straight.
> Do not be wise in your own eyes.
>
> Proverbs 3:5–7

Our house situation wasn't easy to solve. No one was able to figure it out, and that made the problem last for what seemed like forever. At some point we began to stop trusting in our own ideas of what happened and began asking God for his wisdom to show us. Until we knew what the culprit was, nothing could be fixed. We were deadlocked in a mess.

A friend of ours was puzzled by the whole thing and came over, sure he would find the problem. But, he could not figure it out either. However, as he was walking out our garage, a drop of water, like the first one that fell on my husband's head weeks earlier, landed on my friends brow. He became determined, and after getting a ladder and opening up the garage ceiling, he found a nail that was embedded in a plastic tubing pipe.

End of story—the builder then stood behind the problem, fixing everything, making our house like new. With no money out of our pocket, the house was fitted with new carpet, and new piping, and all was back to normal right before Thanksgiving Day. The Lord made the path straight as we began looking to him rather than spinning in circles.

Where are you today? God knows the details of your current hardship. He desires to see you through to the end.

When you are in the middle of a problem, stop to ask these questions:

- What is the problem? (In this case, mine was a house disaster.)
- What are my options? (I can scream, fret, or stay calm.)
- Which one will I choose? (I want to scream but will choose to stay calm.)
- When will I start? (The moment I realize I really do have a choice.)

Can you try, just for today, just for the next five minutes even, to focus on God's ability to see you through? Remember, you often can't choose your circumstances, but you can choose how you will live in them. Being overwhelmed is a choice.

Overwhelmed means:

1. to flood over: engulf
2. to overcome utterly: as by physical or emotional force
3. to turn over: upset[2]

When was the last time you felt engulfed by a problem or pain? Maybe it's right now. Perhaps the emotional force is upsetting you so much that you are barely making it through the day. You spin the facts, fret over the outcome, worry more than trust. For the record, that is what it looks like to be overwhelmed. And believe it or not, even though it feels we must be overwhelmed, as if there is no other option, the truth is there is always a choice.

> We should battle through our moods, feelings, and emotions.
>
> Oswald Chambers[3]

The opposite of being overwhelmed is to surrender the current situation to God. Surrender is an important step in trusting. Surrender:

1. to give up control or possession of to another
2. to give oneself over: to yield[4]

Surrendering a problem to the Lord is a choice. It's intentional. We must stop and purposely give it to him. It's more than just wishing he would take it from us; it's knowing we have given it over to him. As Christians, we often lean on our own wisdom and understanding, much more than we would like to admit. "We do not believe God, we enthrone common sense and tack the name of God on to it. We lean on our own understanding, instead of trusting God with all our hearts."[5]

Think again about the last thing that overwhelmed you. What would it look like to live in peace instead of turmoil? Do you think it's a viable option? When we are overwhelmed, we are to surrender whatever is overwhelming us to God.

> From the end of the earth will I cry unto thee, when my heart is overwhelmed: lead me to the rock that is higher than I.
>
> Psalm 61:2 KJV

Your current problem or challenge can overcome you. It can get you in an emotional grip that might make it difficult for you to trust God in your situation. Often when we are in that emotional place, we completely give ourselves over to being upset.

Is this how you want to spend today? Do you want to surrender to the emotional grip of distress? Is this how you want to live until there is a solution to your situation? I bet not. There is a better way.

> May the LORD answer you when you are in distress;
> may the name of the God of Jacob protect you. . . .
> Now this I know:
>     The LORD gives victory to his anointed.
> He answers him from his heavenly sanctuary
>     with the victorious power of his right hand.
> Some trust in chariots and some in horses,
>     but we trust in the name of the LORD our God.
>
> Psalm 20:1, 6–7

**In my meantime place, I am learning . . .**

_____

_____

_____

_____

_____

_____

**In my meantime place, God is requiring me to . . .**

_____

_____

_____

_____

_____

_____

### Prayer

*Lord, I want to learn to trust you. Living overwhelmed is easy, but I want to try something different, something that requires faith. It is my prayer that faith will be pleasing to you in every way. Teach me, Jesus, to trust you. Amen.*

# 3

# The Forgotten Promise

## *You Are Not Alone*

For we do not have a high priest who is unable to sympathize with our weakness.

Hebrews 4:15

The rain whipped in front of the windshield, making it difficult to see the road ahead. But as we stopped at a red light, things got a little clearer, and the bright lights of the Christmas sign at the corner church caught my eye. "Welcome, Prince of Peace!" stood out, shining through the downpour. And with the movement of the wind, it almost seemed like that little sign was flashing its small lights, sending a message on that soggy December night—a night when people undoubtedly were taking cover in their homes, at a time of year when suicide hotlines are busier than ever, depression soars, and the most wonderful time of the year is often seen as much less than wonderful. Truth is, some people just try to get through Christmas and get on with a new year that will hopefully be better than the one that just ended.

As my thoughts flashed through a year that had been filled with illness, relationship drama, and personal uncertainty, I thought, *Yes, oh yes, I welcome you. I will swing open the door for you, Prince of Peace. Prince of Peace, I need you!*

It's not that I hadn't heard God addressed by that title before, because I had heard it many times over the years. But like a worn-out pair of shoes, those words had lost their shine. I don't know about you, but I have often taken them for granted, giving little attention to the significance of what they could mean to us—if we believed them to be true. The calm is always best after the storm, and it's often in that calm that we rebuild. For me, after a year of hard things, it was time for me to reevaluate where I was placing my trust and why I often lacked real peace. It occurred to me that I had forgotten the promise of the prophet Isaiah:

> For to us a child is born,
>     to us a son is given,
>     and the government will be on his shoulders.
> And he will be called
>     Wonderful Counselor, Mighty God,
>     Everlasting Father, Prince of Peace.
>
> Isaiah 9:6

We are familiar with the catchphrases of Christmas—words on greeting cards and banners. But just as we don't place too much stock in Frosty the Snowman, maybe we are guilty of not paying close enough attention to the words in God's Word, words that describe the one God sent to us.

Wonderful Counselor

Mighty God

Everlasting Father
Prince of Peace

Let me sum up these four titles here: we are not alone!

These words introduce us to the one God sent to be in our lives. It's as if God wrote his own Christmas card with a promise of what he would be to his people.

Isaiah said, "There will be no more gloom for those who were in distress. . . . The people walking in darkness have seen a great light; on those living in the land of deep darkness a light has dawned. You have enlarged the nation and increased their joy" (9:1–3). Surely this did not mean there would be no more problems, but it is clear that because of who Christ came to be, joy would be increased, gloom would be alleviated, and life would be different.

My friend Kari West speaks of this:

> Too often it escapes our notice that the greatest sermon ever preached took place not in a brightly lit, ornately decorated, crowded cathedral, but in a plain farm field of a poor country beneath a dark sky in front of a few ordinary shepherds. Both the Good News and the best gift arrived at night. . . . Into our own dark December comes this undeserved and unbelievable love gift from the Father. You and I are accepted just as we are—moody or merry; rich or poor; married, widowed or divorced. . . . This gift comes with an eternal, unchanging, non-negotiable, non-refundable guarantee.[1]

Yes, Jesus, Immanuel, is with us—and is bigger than anything we can possibly go through. Jesus spoke of peace and the absence of living in the distress that the world can bring. He promised never to leave his people alone. He promised us a comforter.

> But the Counselor, the Holy Spirit, whom the Father will send in my name, will teach you all things and will remind you of

everything I have said to you. Peace I leave with you; my peace I give you. I do not give to you as the world gives. Do not let your hearts be troubled and do not be afraid.

John 14:26–27

## Prince of Peace

There is a clear indication in the above passage that Jesus promised peace and that this peace can be ours . . . *if*. What is the condition? We are responsible for where we allow our hearts to settle, dwell, stay for the day. If we let peace in, not allowing the negative habit of being troubled and stressed to rule us, we will have the peace that Jesus said is bigger and better than anything the world can give us.

I think it's time to sit on the edge of our seats and take note here. Maybe you and I read the Christmas greeting and throw the meaning away. Then we wonder, in the middle of our storms, why it seems our umbrella is leaking, our feet are freezing, and there is no shelter. The shelter is there all right. It's just that we have become immune to the words of truth and fail to nestle up under that mighty shelter and find peace under it.

If God is with us, if God is bigger than our problems, if God is mighty, faithful, and true, then we can receive his gift of grace in the form of mental peace. But the catch is that you and I have a part to play in this. We can't stand on the street corner ranting and raving about our latest crisis and expect a wave of peace to wash over us! We have something to do. We need to make a choice and discipline our mind and emotions. This choice is a spiritual practice that changes the condition and climate of our mind and attitude.

1. We choose to believe God is in control.
2. We allow the reality of peace based on his control to enter our mind.

3. We choose to push out all worry and concern for tomorrow's outcome, trusting God this day.
4. We continually fill our mind with the truth: God is bigger than this problem. We focus, often several times a day.

As I sat staring through a blurry windshield at the brightly lit sign, those words, "Welcome, Prince of Peace!" struck me in a new way. The phrase was no longer a cliché and far more than a Christmas greeting on a church sign. No, above all these things, it was a welcoming of a promise into my life.

Jesus promised to leave us with his peace . . . period. Such peace is not dependent on my situation, controlled by my circumstances, or constrained by how other people's poor choices affect me. Simply stated, Jesus is the Prince of Peace. And that is the greatest promise of all.

We can have many things in life, but they mean nothing without peace of mind. If our mind is jumbled and anxious, even the fanciest house or car will not be enough. If our mind is not settled and our heart is filled with fear, even having all we ever hoped for will not fulfill us. There is something, an intangible, that can lower our blood pressure, increase our serotonin level, lift our mood, and give us a good night's rest. Peace. It is the secret to our contentment. And it is found in relationship with Jesus Christ.

> Trust Me with every fiber of your being! What I can accomplish in and through you is proportioned to how much you depend on me. . . . I care as much about your tiny trust-steps through daily life as about your dramatic leaps of faith. You may think that no one notices, but the One who is always beside you sees everything—and rejoices. Consistently trusting in Me is vital to flourishing in My Presence.
>
> Sarah Young[2]

We like to say we trust while we are wringing our hands in fear and worry, but it's time to make an honest evaluation about where we are and how we live while waiting for a problem to be resolved. We might trust God with our salvation, our eternal destination, the overall benefits of knowing him. But do we trust him when the tire is flat, the kids are sick, the marriage is struggling?

## Wonderful Counselor

I often begin my speaking engagements with a quote I once heard: "If it's free, it's advice. If you pay for it, it's counseling. If it works, it's a miracle!" That always makes me smile because I have received plenty of advice and have had more than my share of counseling, but what I have always needed is the miracle that only God can perform deep within me. He is our Wonderful Counselor!

The word *wonderful* means astonishing or marvelous or exceptionally fine. Often my life does not match that definition, but that is when I must draw from who Christ is and what he came to be: my wonderful, astonishing, marvelous, exceptionally fine counselor.

In the middle of every storm or trouble, we need advice and guidance, and we must get into the practice of asking God to give us what we need, tell us what to do, and guide us down the road that will lead us to where he is taking us. The word *counselor* comes from the Hebrew word *yaats*, which means to advise, resolve, guide, purpose. With those definitions I can say, "He is my wonderful Advisor, my wonderful Resolver, my wonderful Guide and my wonderful Purpose!"[3]

A while ago a friend found out that her husband of twenty years was living a secret life. She was devastated, as any of us would be. She didn't want to throw away the past twenty years, nor did she want to devastate their daughter with a divorce, so she chose instead to believe—actually for the first time—that Jesus came to be a mighty God for people like her and her husband, people lost in the grip of pain and addiction, people with no way out on their own. Believing this truth was her personal miracle. It gave her stamina and perspective to face the daunting challenge ahead of them. It would be a long road, but Jesus would be her counselor and he would prove himself to be a mighty God on their behalf.

## Everlasting Father

Most of us would like to be wrapped in Daddy's arms when life is hard. Even if we didn't have that kind of security growing up, we probably can all relate to wishing we did. Fortunately, Jesus is our Everlasting Father. He never changes. He is timeless. Our earthly fathers may have disappointed us, but God never will. No matter what your earthly father has been in your life, your heavenly Father is greater still. Jesus contrasts earthly parents with himself when he said:

> Which of you, if your son asks for bread, will give him a stone? Or if he asks for a fish, will give him a snake? If you, then, though you are evil, know how to give good gifts to your children, how much more will your Father in heaven give good gifts to those who ask him!
>
> Matthew 7:9–11

*Everlasting* comes from the Hebrew root *ad*, which means duration, continue, and advance. I can rejoice that God is a Father who will stay with me for the duration of the journey, the entire battle of each problem, and throughout my lifetime. He is a Father who gives the advance or the next step.

In real life, we lose our fathers, our mothers, and those who have guided our lives. But it's comforting to realize that though we can be without parents here on earth, we are never without our Father in heaven. He is from everlasting to everlasting, and this promise is more than a string of nice thoughts. It's truth.

One of the definitions I found for *everlasting* is "around the clock." He is my around-the-clock Father! He never sleeps. He cares for you and me nonstop! Some women have experienced rejection or abandonment. The pain of such an experience is real and is often carried around for years. We must remember that God never abandons. Though people can inflict real pain in our lives, God desires to fill us with peace as we realize that he is with us 24/7.

## Mighty God

*Mighty* comes from the Hebrew word *gibbor*, which means powerful, warrior, champion, chief, giant, strong. With all of that in mind we can say, "God is powerful, a warrior, and a champion. He is my giant God and my strong God in the middle of my current problem."

We often don't reflect much on who God is and how mighty he is. If we did, we would gain strength and peace. Instead in our wimpy faith moments we unknowingly reduce God to a puny powerless cliché in our life. Time to turn that around.

Recently I sat in Psalm 23 for a few months. I read, memorized, reflected, and meditated on those six verses. It was then that I was challenged to look at the way God mightily works in our lives. He is always involved:

- he makes me . . .
- he leads me . . .
- he guides me . . .

- he restores me . . .
- he is with me . . .
- he anoints me . . .
- he provides for me . . .

And, it all starts out with, "The Lord is my shepherd." The Lord *is*. Who is he? This is what we need to focus on. He is a mighty God, a warrior for his people, healer, deliverer, comforter, counselor, creator, all powerful . . . we can go on and on, and we should. Today reflect on those five words, "the Lord is my shepherd," and now make it six words: "the Lord is my mighty shepherd." Thank him for how big and great, all-powerful and sovereign he is!

## The Keeper of Our Welfare

*Prince* is from the Hebrew word *sar*, which means a head person, chief, captain, or keeper. Peace is from the Hebrew *shalom*, which means welfare, health, prosperity, and peace. Get this with me: we can call Christ the Prince of Peace, or we can say that he is the keeper of our welfare![4] He is the keeper of our well-being. He is truly everything we need, and that is a promise that will get us through the meantime.

- The meantime is real—we need a plan for it.
- The meantime begins with a problem—being overwhelmed by it is optional.
- The meantime must be lived out with a promise—Jesus promises to be our keeper in the middle of every storm.

Sometimes in the middle of a real-life problem, thinking of God, big and high above us, makes his help seem out of reach. If God seems lofty and too busy for your current problem, consider each name given to the Son and address him by that name. How about calling him your Wonderful Counselor? Your Prince of Peace? Your Mighty God? Or your Everlasting Father? And don't forget that he promised to always be with us.

Too often we forget how big and mighty our God is. And far too often, we exchange our worry and fear for the peace that is ours in him. Let's try something different. It just might change things.

**In my meantime place, I am learning . . .**

_____

_____

_____

_____

_____

_____

**In my meantime place, God is requiring me to . . .**

_____

_____

_____

_____

_____

_____

### Prayer

*Lord, you sent Jesus to be my peace. He is the promise of everything I need to live this life and the one to come. Too often I try to take on my challenges alone. Forgive me. Help me to remember who Christ came to be and the power of that in my daily life. Let me know Jesus as my Wonderful Counselor, my Mighty God, my Everlasting Father, and my Prince of Peace. I desire to trust you, Lord God, with all that is within me. I want to honor you by trusting you while in the middle of each and every circumstance. Amen.*

# 4

## God Holds You Together

*Even When Things Are Falling Apart*

For I know that through your prayers and God's provision of
the Spirit of Jesus Christ what has happened to me will turn
out for my deliverance. I eagerly expect and hope that I will in
no way be ashamed, but will have sufficient courage.

Philippians 1:19–20

The worst part of the meantime is that in the long stretch of
middle space we can be easily tempted to live only to make
the pain go away. We each have our own means of making the
pain go away, but rather than avoid the pain, it is best to face
the pain, knowing that the God who made us is with us in the
pain and that the painful place will ultimately turn out for our
good and growth.

In the early years of my Christian walk, I began to sense a
stirring in my heart—a call to ministry. Even though I was young

and inexperienced, I had a strong desire to fulfill whatever God's intent was for my life.

Life complied with this call, and I married a pastor. My life was filled to the brim with what we call ministry. Then my little world was blown apart by divorce, shame, and feelings that God was done with me. I was devastated and felt lost. I wish I could tell you that I sought God day and night at that point. But I didn't. I got angry, acted out, played the passive-aggressive role with God, and did some pretty stupid things.

The unfortunate part of a life crisis is that we don't usually bounce right back. We experience a stretch between the beginning and the end of a problem—and sometimes it lasts for years. Mine did. During those years, we can feel we'll never make it to the other side, that God has left us, that we're on our own.

## Knowing Whose You Are

That was many years ago. These days I have different challenges and have grown up a bit. The challenges are still hard, but the growth has helped me to believe that I am held together by God and that I really do belong to him. And if I truly believe I belong to him and that he ultimately holds me together, then I can trust even when my plan is not in place or I don't understand his.

> He is before all things, and in him all things hold together.
>
> Colossians 1:17

I talk to women from all over the country who desperately need to believe that they too are being held together by something bigger than themselves and something better than their problems.

This year I met a beautiful young woman. She was in turmoil. Her situation was more than she could bear. Everywhere she looked, things seemed to be falling apart—at home, at work, and in her friendships. Day by day, as things seemed to worsen, she forgot not only that God was looking after her and all that concerned her but also that she belonged to him. With all that she was facing, it hardly seemed important to center her thoughts on belonging to God.

But her identity as his makes all the difference. When we forget that we belong to a God who is big, mighty, faithful, and always with us, we lose heart, hope, and faith in the bigger picture.

> We look at this Son and see the God who cannot be seen. We look at this Son and see God's original purpose in everything created. For everything, absolutely everything, above and below, visible and invisible, rank after rank after rank of angels—everything got started in him and finds its purpose in him. He was there before any of it came into existence and holds it all together right up to this moment.
>
> Colossians 1:15–17 Message

> God will send his forces out where we have failed to do so. He will keep watch so that we will not be tripped up again by the same failures, as would undoubtedly happen if he were not our rear guard.
>
> Oswald Chambers[1]

It's easy to forget we are being held together by God's mighty grip. We all forget from time to time, and when we do, we open ourselves up to a real enemy whose goal is to get us to live apart from God and who we are as his.

The Bible tells us that this enemy is a thief who lurks in the backdrop of our story. The thief is a permanent fixture in the human condition here on earth. We are told that he prowls about as a roaring lion, seeking to devour us, and that he is the accuser of the brethren—with the express job of lying to us, accusing us of not belonging to God, and discouraging us from looking up into the eyes of the one who loves us and calls us his own.

This same enemy wants nothing more than for you and me to misunderstand who we are, forget who holds us together, and give up. If he can get us to believe we are on our own, like orphans struggling through life, he will win, and we will believe we have been left to figure things out by ourselves.

The enemy wants us to give up on walking with God when the going gets rough. But the truth is we have a God who carries us, leads us, protects us, and uses the rough patches in life to advance us. The liar does not want us to know this truth, because if we do, we won't be as easily defeated. If we know that we are "kept women," we will not be looking for answers on the enemy's turf. Rather, we will learn to trust the one who keeps us in his arms.

| God's Plan | The Thief's Plan |
| --- | --- |
| To give you the security of belonging | To keep you searching for security |
| To give you a foundation for life | To have you build your life on happiness |
| To do good to you | To rob all good from you |
| To be your strength | To tempt you to rely on self strength |
| To be your provision | To keep you worrying about what you need |
| To be your rest | To keep you running |
| To give you faith | To keep you in unbelief, doubt, and fear |

When we believe the truth, we stand taller, love deeper, rest easier, and are more productive in every season of our existence. But when we don't believe the truth, we shrink down to the smallness of living only in our self, reduced to settling for insecurities, fearful dread, and constant worry about the possible outcomes of our problems. When we live with a mistaken identity, we miss the best life God has for us.

I find it particularly interesting the way Paul defines who he is at the beginning of Philippians. He doesn't say, "Hey, this is Paul, the one who was thrown unfairly into prison while serving God's people." Instead, he identifies who he is in accordance with whose he is.

Paul and Timothy, servants of Christ Jesus.

Philippians 1:1

This might not sound like much to you, but it is huge. Why is this so important? Because what defines us will be the very thing that drives us. When you are in the meantime, spiritual definition is vital.

The word *servants* refers to those slaves who were totally possessed by another. The central thought is that of belonging to God. The resulting act is complete surrender. The first step to finding peace in the overwhelming frustrations of the meantime is surrender, and a prerequisite to surrender is understanding whose we are and how we are loved and provided for.

You are not your own; you were bought at a price.

1 Corinthians 6:19–20

We have been bought through the death of Christ. His blood paid the entrance into a new life in the Spirit. Our lives are different. We still have problems, but we now face them from a different place. We face our problems from a place of those redeemed by God, owned by God, and loved by God. This ownership piece of the gospel makes all the difference, but we often pay no attention to it.

Several years ago, I needed to know that I belonged to something greater than myself. I felt immune to the basics in Scripture. To be honest, they probably bored me a bit at the time. The sad thing is, I am not alone. Many who have been around church or

Christian circles for a while become immune to the basic truths that can change their lives. Why? Maybe because we have heard them over and over. They seem too basic, too simple, too cliché. So in our search for something more, we overlook the foundations. We don't give them the attention they deserve. We end up living our life based on doing things rather than being his while living through things.

When we understand we are his, our life changes because we desire to live a life worthy of that calling. We begin to respond differently when the foundation of our identity is solid. We actually begin living in the truth of what Christ came to be in us, through us, and for us.

Take a look at truth on the subject:

To all who did receive him, to those who believed in his name, he gave the right to become children of God—children born not of natural descent, nor of human decision or a husband's will, but born of God.

John 1:12–13

Know that the LORD is God.
It is he who made us, and we are his;
we are his people, the sheep of his pasture.

Psalm 100:3

He calls his own sheep by name and leads them out. When he has brought out all his own, he goes on ahead of them, and his sheep follow him because they know his voice.

John 10:3–4

The thief comes only to steal and kill and destroy; I have come that they may have life, and have it to the full. I am the good shepherd. The good shepherd lays down his life for the sheep.

John 10:10–11

As we move through the teachings in Philippians, we will discover some essential truths for our daily path. We will also see someone very different from us. We will see Paul, who had the ability to view life through a different lens. He was experiencing the reality of Christ's love, the reality of what Christ's death meant to him personally, the reality of living life with joy no matter what his circumstances were. And though he lived many years ago, we would be wise to pay attention to and learn from him!

This different life begins with the foundation of a proper identity and knowing our life is secure in God's hand. How does this make a difference? It is a stance of daily surrender, trust, and purpose. It is believing that we are each a part of a bigger story—God's story. If we remind ourselves every day that the day really isn't about *us* but about his work and way *in us*, our attitude toward the meantime places in life will change.

Paul was confident of Christ's ownership of the Christians in Philippi. He continually encouraged them to believe the truth and be complete and content in that truth. He encourages us to live a life of trust in the middle of any mishap or problem. His message to us is this: you are God's, so live in that identity.

> I have been crucified with Christ and I no longer live, but Christ lives in me. The life I now live in the body, I live by faith in the Son of God, who loved me and gave himself for me.
>
> Galatians 2:20

Identity:

1. The condition or fact of being a certain person or thing and recognizable as such.
2. The condition or fact of being the same as something else: sameness.[2]

Where are you today? What are you facing? May I suggest that you remember who you are and whose you are? May I suggest that you don't brush it aside one more time but instead hold on to the truth of your new identity in Christ and allow the truth to make all the difference in your capacity for hope in your current situation?

## Develop Your Trust in God

You are hit with a situation, a problem, a trial, a waiting space—and you don't like it, it's not fun, and you are not comfortable. You have a choice. You can forget whose you are and try to fix things on your own, or you can focus on the truth that God is still on the throne and the Lord over your life. He is in control. He holds you together.

In the meantime, pay attention to his still, small voice. He might not give a direct answer to your situation, but if you focus on Scripture about who he is and his faithfulness, you will get just enough light in the dark to illuminate the step you are on. It's limited, but it's enough.

Finally, do not obsess over knowing the plan. Instead, we must trust without knowing the end result or how God will use this situation to further our growth. Live one day at a time, one step at a time, and listen to his leading.

Going through trials is like spiritual weight training. The weight of the problem builds endurance in the faith muscle of our soul. Some problems are brief, and some go on for years. All require trust. God desires to lift us above our situations and give us true peace. His peace he gives to you—and me.

Hang in there. God is with you!

**In my meantime place, I am learning . . .**

_____

_____

_____

_____

**In my meantime place, God is requiring me to . . .**

_____

_____

_____

_____

### Prayer

_Lord, it is easy to forget my connection to you and yours to me. I get up and get going, doing my daily routine, and often forget that in you I am a new living being. My life is not my own, and I need to be reminded of that all the time. As I come today and remember that I belong to you, I pray that you would make that truth more real to me than ever before. Please don't let me live a life of identity theft, but rather give me the grace to live a life being completely sure of who I am and whose I am. And may this knowing make all the difference in how I live my life. Amen._

# 5

# God Is Always at Work

## *He Is in the Details*

For to me, to live is Christ and to die is gain. If I am to go on living in the body, this will mean fruitful labor for me.

Philippians 1:21–22

A mother took her little boy to a piano concert. Upon arrival she saw a friend and started visiting. The restless little boy wandered off, and soon the lights went out for the concert to begin. The mother, looking to find her son, glanced toward the stage and saw her little boy pecking out "Twinkle, Twinkle, Little Star." The young mom watched in shock as the master musician walked out on stage and whispered quietly to her son to keep playing. And the little boy did.

As he continued, the pianist played with his left hand the bass and with his right hand a beautiful running obbligato. The audience was mesmerized by the beauty of the child's efforts as they were embellished by the power and skill of the master musician.

As we struggle to live, plucking out our notes to simple tunes, God our master says, "Don't quit, keep playing, keep trying. Keep going and keep growing." And out of our life come the beauty and strength of his power and work. While we are alive, our lives are to be lived for Christ and through Christ's power at work within us.

## A Good Work

The concept of Christ empowering the Christian permeates the entire letter of Philippians. And like the little boy and the musician at the recital, Christ comes alongside us and works in us and through us. We might not be able to see him, but he is there.

In his letter to his friends in Philippi, Paul talks about God's work in those who have received Christ—those who have surrendered to his life in them.

> Being confident of this, that he who began a good work in you
> will carry it on to completion until the day of Christ Jesus.
>
> Philippians 1:6

Early in his letter, Paul introduces one of Christianity's most dynamic and compelling concepts: God is at work in human lives. This verse stresses God's divine work in an individual life and introduces us to the secret of Paul's spiritual power. Paul was filled with power because God was at work in him. Later on he will say, "For it is God who works in you to will and to act in order to fulfill his good purpose" (Phil. 2:13).

Stop right now and think about this truth. Repeat the truth that God is at work in you this very moment. God is working in you. God will carry you and his work in you to the finish line. God will complete his work in you.

> Now to him who is able to do immeasurably more than all we ask or imagine, according to his power that is at work within us.

Ephesians 3:20

Paul was confident that God was all powerful and that Christ's power was sufficient to complete him. What do you need from the Father today? What work do you need to believe his power is capable of accomplishing in you? Are you confident of his power or just wishful for it?

Paul is not saying that we may not fall down from time to time, but he is saying that we don't have to stay there. We do our part—not a perfect performance but a continual surrender and submission to God—and God will be faithful to complete his work in us.

But sometimes it seems God has forgotten my situation. As the waves of life crash down on me and the undercurrent of the problem threatens to suck me into the deep and drown me, I tend to forget. I don't forget that there is a God, but I do forget that he hasn't forgotten me and that contrary to what it looks like, he is always at work. Always! As Oswald Chambers says, "We can all see God in exceptional things, but it requires the growth of spiritual discipline to see God in every detail."[1]

There are many stories throughout Scripture about those who had every reason to think God had forgotten them. Imagine Joseph, an innocent kid who was his father's favorite. Naturally, his brothers were jealous and began to plot against him. They tossed their little brother into a well, and if that wasn't bad enough, he was pulled up only to be sold into slavery. All this at the hands of his brothers, whom he undoubtedly trusted.

His story goes from bad to worse, and Joseph ends up in prison. The worst part of this story, in my opinion, is that Joseph was betrayed and hurt by people he loved. Many of us know that story line, don't we? We might not be thrown into a well, sold into slavery, or locked away in prison, but for many of us the hardest part of trusting God is that the very thing that happened to us happened at the hands of people we love.

I used to get hung up in the fact that God allowed such and such to happen to me. Why? Why would God allow that? Then, with some sense in my pea brain, I began to realize that it wasn't God hurting me but people's choices. God does not make us live as robots. He gives us free will to choose. Often others' choices hurt us. Does this stop the hand of God in our life? Can other people ruin his plan? Remember this: God is always working in you.

If we are going to be women who trust God, we must believe that he is working in *all* things, despite the poor decisions or choices others make that affect us. It's quite possible that God will use a poor choice on someone else's part to redirect us into his fuller plan for our life.

Still, we all know about life going from bad to worse, don't we? This is life. But we can learn to live above it. We can learn to live in joy despite what is happening around us. Joy is much different from happiness. Joy is a contrast to happiness, running deeper and stronger. Joy is the quiet assurance that God is at work in our life and that he will be there no matter what. Happiness depends on happenings, but joy depends on Christ.

When life hits you upside the head, know this: the God who began a good work in you is still working. Oftentimes his best work takes place when things are not easy.

Look at Philippians 1:6 in a few other versions:

There has never been the slightest doubt in my mind that the God who started this great work in you would keep at it and bring it to a flourishing finish on the very day Christ Jesus appears.

Message

I feel sure that the one who has begun his good work in you will go on developing it until the day of Jesus Christ.

Phillips

And I am convinced and sure of this very thing, that He Who began a good work in you will continue until the day of Jesus Christ [right up to the time of His return], developing [that good work] and perfecting and bringing it to full completion in you.

AMP

- God's goal is a flourishing finish.
- God's goal is to develop us.
- God's plan is bringing full completion into our lives.

## Paul's Secret

Paul was no stranger to less-than-perfect situations. Persecution seemed to be his middle name, and the prison cell was the place he kept learning to call home sweet home. I am amazed that a person could live through all that he lived through. Interestingly, he didn't just live through it all—he thrived through it. He developed, grew, loved, and praised God in the middle of all his life happenings. How could he do this?

Paul had a little secret up his sleeve: he knew God was at work in his life, regardless of what it looked like around him. In the meantime places of life, our circumstances do not feel loving and often don't seem kind. By nature of the meantime, things usually appear frustrating. And who better than Paul to write about this. He was in the meantime, and it was mean, lonely, and unfair. It was in this place that he continued to live as one loved by God.

> The LORD is trustworthy in all he promises
>> and faithful in all he does.
> The LORD upholds all who fall
>> and lifts up all who are bowed down.
> The eyes of all look to you,
>> and you give them their food at the proper time.
> You open your hand
>> and satisfy the desires of every living thing.
> The LORD is righteous in all his ways
>> and faithful in all he does.
> The LORD is near to all who call on him,
>> to all who call on him in truth.
> He fulfills the desires of those who fear him;
>> he hears their cry and saves them.
>
> Psalm 145:13–19

It's important for us to realize that things happen *to* us so something greater can happen *in* us. God is always at work, and it's an inside job!

You may not understand your situation, but you can believe in God and his work in you this very moment. Obey the God who loves you and yield yourself to him. That is how to find more joy than you could ever imagine.

**In my meantime place, I am learning . . .**

_____

_____

_____

_____

_____

**In my meantime place, God is requiring me to . . .**

---

---

---

---

---

### Prayer

*Heavenly Father, I want to thank you for working in my life. I might not see you and often don't feel you, but I believe by faith that you are working and you are developing me. You, Lord, complete me, satisfy me, protect me, and bring me into all that you have designed for me. Have your way in me today. Give me strength to face the rough spots in my current journey. I need to believe you are orchestrating a work in me. Thank you for the promise that you are working. Teach me your ways. Amen.*

# 6

# Suffering Is a Part of Life

*God Knows the Language of Your Tears*

Whatever happens, conduct yourselves in a manner worthy of the gospel of Christ. . . . For it has been granted to you on behalf of Christ not only to believe in him, but also to suffer for him.

Philippians 1:27, 29

The doorbell rang, but nothing could have prepared her for what was on the other side of the door. Two policemen stood larger than life in her entryway. It was only nine in the morning. What could they possibly want? Her mind raced but was stopped short by one of the police officers addressing her.

"Yes, what is it?" she asked as her heart stopped at the possibilities.

"Your daughter was in a car accident earlier this morning." At the solemn announcement, something in her heart knew that her daughter was no longer here. And before she could gather her thoughts or form her words, she was out the door en route with a neighbor and friend to identify her precious twenty-three-year-old girl at the county morgue.

One look was all it took. A mother knows her child. It was her. How could this be? Her girl was on her way for a visit, coming to spend the weekend with her mother. Instead, a heartsick mother was now spending the weekend calling friends and relatives and experiencing a grief that was deeper and more painful than anything she had ever felt before.

The next few days were filled with details—the service, the flowers, the memorial. Her daughter's friends came to help her with the planning. They also provided an answer to a question she had about her daughter. The coroner had given her a bracelet that her daughter was wearing when she died. Having never seen it before, she was puzzled by its meaning. It had a shiny, sterling silver heart on it engraved with one word: *his*. Naturally, any mother would want to know what that simple word meant. Had she met someone? Was she in love? Engaged? The curiosity almost enveloped her while she waited to ask her daughter's roommates.

Yes, it was true. She had met someone. She wanted her mother to meet him too. But it wasn't a guy from college; it was Jesus Christ, whom she had received as her Lord and Savior a month earlier when she had attended a women's retreat with her friends. This visit was specifically to introduce her mother to faith in Christ. Instead, three roommates were sharing the gospel with a grieving, heartsick mom.

A few years later, I met this mom at a women's retreat where I was speaking. She noticed my book table and the same type of silver bracelets. She figured that maybe every Christian speaker sells them and shrugged it off. At the close of the retreat, I shared my mother's last words to me: "Live like it's real, because it is!" It was then that she knew I was the woman who had spoken the night her daughter became a Christian, and I was the one she had gotten the bracelet from. It all became clear as she remembered her daughter's friends telling a grieving crowd at the memorial service to live like it's real.

As women were leaving the retreat, she found me and asked for a picture together. As another woman snapped a Kodak moment, she hugged me tightly. Realizing this was more than a picture, I leaned back and looked her in the eyes. She pulled a bracelet from her pocket. It wasn't new or polished, but it was a treasure she carried with her. She told me about her daughter and thanked me. The picture we took together is in a double frame on her mantel—on one side, she and her daughter, on the other, the two of us. It serves as a reminder that through the most horrible suffering of her life, she found Jesus. I am humbled to be on her mantel. I am awestruck by how suffering, as hard as it was, moved this woman to a place deeper than she had ever been.

> I believe that loss and emptiness and confusion often give way to new fullness and wisdom.
>
> Shauna Niequist[1]

The apostle Paul speaks of suffering:

> There's also suffering for him. And the suffering is as much a gift as the trusting.
>
> Philippians 1:29 Message

Some of us are afraid of our own emotions. We don't want to feel pain. Who does? Pain, however, is a part of life, as is suffering. Pain comes in all sizes and for a variety of reasons. Suffering is usually a result of some pain. Today you might be in a place of pain. You might be experiencing the death of your dreams, a loved one, or a well-oiled plan, the death of your good health, your expectations, or a cherished friendship. Loss is all around us, and loss brings a painful chapter of suffering into our lives. Paul, knowing this, embraced the pain and leaned into the suffering. How did he do this? By focusing on what is ahead, the promise of heaven, and the renewing that happens here and now—the renewal that makes us more spiritually tuned in.

Kari West writes, "Unrelenting pain has a way of getting our attention and forcing us to our knees—whether thrust upon us by a betrayal, the death of someone close, or other losses. The first thing most of us seek is an end to the suffering or, at least, momentary relief. What we really need is mercy. Mercy to bear us up when emotions weigh us down. Mercy is a God-given gift that you and I do not deserve. The way God shows mercy during life's emotional moments include:

- When tears are the only language you know, God hears.
- When darkness envelops your way, God sees.
- When pain forces you off course, God stabilizes.
- When loss weighs you down, God comforts.
- When grief suspends your progress and saps hope, God remains."[2]

We do not lose heart. Though outwardly we are wasting away, yet inwardly we are being renewed day by day.

2 Corinthians 4:16

Not one of us would want to face what this mother faced. None of us can understand the death of a child or unexpected loss. This is where trust comes in. We live in a world that has loss and suffering. We must learn how to live in it by trusting God and having faith that he is with us.

Let's review what we have been learning so far:

- When bad things happen, God is still in control and is still with you.
- Live one day at a time, one step at a time, and listen for his leading.
- Remember that God does not always explain the plan, even when you are in it.
- Things happen *to* you so something greater can happen *in* you. Your current situation may be moving you into greater places of spiritual health and freedom.

**In my meantime place, I am learning . . .**

_____

_____

_____

_____

_____

**In my meantime place, God is requiring me to . . .**

_____

_____

_____

_____

_____

**Prayer**

*Heavenly Father, I thank you that you are a God of mercy. We suffer; you comfort. We feel like we will fall; you hold us. Without you where could we go, how could we trust? Suffering is a part of life. Paul knew it, and I know it. I just don't want to embrace it. Help me to yield to you in everything I go through. Jesus, be with me and grant me your mercy today. Amen.*

71

# 7

# Develop a New View of Suffering

## *Difficult Circumstances Can Change You*

Have the same mindset as Christ Jesus. . . . He made himself nothing by taking the very nature of a servant, being made in human likeness. And being found in appearance as a man, he humbled himself by becoming obedient to death—even death on a cross!

Philippians 2:5, 7–8

I was doing back-to-back weekends at the same retreat center, so the second weekend I knew what to expect. It would be colder than I had thought it would be, darker at night than I had expected it to be, and it would probably rain—none of which I had prepared for the first time around. Naturally, the second weekend I came armed with warmer clothes, a flashlight, an umbrella, and boots.

My friend Ali, who was assisting me for the weekend, came prepared too. She even thought of bringing a night-light for our cabin—well, not a night-light exactly. She was more creative than that. She brought a glow stick. You know, the kind of thing you see at fairs and concerts. Once it is snapped and shaken a bit, it comes to life with a beautiful colored glow that lights up the area.

The first night I woke up and couldn't get back to sleep. I stared at the glow stick and marveled at how bright one little stick could be. I smiled as I thought of its benefit as a true night-light. Then it hit me. In order for this little stick to be used as a bright and shining light, it had to be snapped and shaken.

The same is true for us, and the snapping of a human life often happens as circumstances break us down. It doesn't feel good while it is happening. Who wants to be snapped and shaken? But this breaking and shaking that happens while we are in the meantime places of life produces something good and beautiful in us later.

## Broken to Be Beautiful

Paul undoubtedly was shaken up when he was treated unfairly. He was just human. He wasn't the Messiah; he wasn't supernatural. Like us, he was just trying to live out his faith in the Lord Jesus Christ. His life had hardships. We know this because he talked about them to encourage the Christians in his time to keep looking to Jesus, hanging in there with hope, and believing in the outcome of God's faithfulness.

> But we have this treasure in jars of clay to show that this all-surpassing power is from God and not from us. We are hard pressed on every side, but not crushed; perplexed, but not in despair; persecuted, but not abandoned; struck down, but not destroyed. We always carry around in our body the death of Jesus, so that the life of Jesus may also be revealed in our body.

For we who are alive are always being given over to death for Jesus' sake, so that his life may also be revealed in our mortal body. So then, death is at work in us, but life is at work in you.

2 Corinthians 4:7–12

Paul was:

- hard pressed on every side
- perplexed
- persecuted
- struck down

I am not sure I want to sign up for that discipleship class. How about you? And then add into the mix that we are given over to death for Jesus's sake. Whoa, that is too heavy and negative for me.

But I am beginning to see that it is not a negative at all. It is life. And though death to self is not popular dinner conversation, it is a true turning point for those who want the abundant life Jesus himself came to give. Life is all about living through him, not living in our own puny strength and ideals. In order for us to shine, we too have to be snapped and shaken.

For it has been granted to you on behalf of Christ not only to believe in him, but also to suffer for him.

Philippians 1:29

So that you may become blameless and pure, "children of God without fault in a warped and crooked generation." Then you will shine among them like stars in the sky.

Philippians 2:15

While we are in the meantime, waiting it out, God is doing something in us. We can't see it, we don't understand it, but it's true. God's work is happening in you—even now. The shaking and breaking will bring you to a place of being a light bearer, with greater intensity than you have ever experienced. If it weren't so, Scripture wouldn't refer to it over and over again—and certainly the apostle Paul wouldn't be drilling it into the hearts of those he loved.

> To say, "I am not my own," is to have reached a high point in my spiritual stature.
>
> Oswald Chambers[1]

It's all in the timing—his timing. We will each be in our situation as long as we need to be.

## When You Can't Control Things

For months I had been in the meantime, wrestling with decisions that affected me but over which I had no control. Still, the issue at hand was looming large, and I wasn't able to change anything about the immediate outcome.

God kept telling me to give it over. I kept giving it over, only to take it back the next time I thought about it. Still, his voice kept asking me to give up the thing that I thought I needed an answer for, assuring me that in his timing I would have the answer.

Then when I least expected it, wasn't even thinking about it, God's answer came as a sweet surprise to me. The very thing I had prayed about happened. It took twelve months, but still, it happened, and the answer was better than anything I had asked for. That is what trusting God is like.

In the middle of the waiting room, there is nothing but silence. The silence makes us want to squirm and makes some of us want to scream. Its deafening quiet tempts us to think God isn't listening, isn't working, and isn't paying attention. But in the meantime of quiet and no answers, God, behind the scenes of our lives, works his finest work in us.

> Now if we are children, then we are heirs—heirs of God and co-heirs with Christ, if indeed we share in his sufferings in order that we may also share in his glory. I consider that our present sufferings are not worth comparing with the glory that will be revealed in us.
>
> Romans 8:17–18

Our present suffering seems unbearable at times, but it is important to learn to praise God even when the situation itself is not praiseworthy—because God is always faithful. The practical side of developing a new view of suffering is to begin praising God. I know it sounds a bit crazy, impractical, maybe fanatical—but it is biblical! Praise releases peace. Praise sets an ambush for the enemy. Praise is a powerful spiritual discipline, a powerful tool, and a strategic path to life and attitude change.

Look what happened when an army praised God in battle.

> They went out at the head of the army, saying: "Give thanks to the LORD, for his love endures forever."
>
> As they began to sing and praise, the LORD set ambushes against the men of Ammon and Moab and Mount Seir who were invading Judah, and they were defeated. . . . And the kingdom of Jehoshaphat was at peace, for his God had given him rest on every side.
>
> 2 Chronicles 20:21–22, 30

What is your current trial, place of suffering, or meantime? Try praising God that even in your pain his love endures forever. Thank him over and over today for his love and faithfulness. I am not asking you to dwell on the problem but to dwell on praising God for who he is.

I bet you will discover something wonderful, even if it's just for today. You will have rest on every side! Try it.

For the next few days schedule time to stop and intentionally thank God and praise him. Try reading something meaningful at each scheduled time. You can do this two to three times a day. Reflect. Thank. Praise. Cast your cares on him. It will take about two to five minutes each scheduled time. The benefits will be priceless.

**In my meantime place, I am learning . . .**

_____

_____

_____

_____

_____

**In my meantime place, God is requiring me to . . .**

_____

_____

_____

_____

_____

**Prayer**

*Lord, help me to have a new view of my suffering and hardships. Though I don't like to be shaken up, I trust you with the work you are doing in me. When I am snapped and shaken, let your light and life shine through me. In your name, amen.*

# 8

# There Is a Plan, Even When It Looks like There Isn't

## God Is in the Outcome

If you have any encouragement from being united with Christ, if any comfort from his love, if any common sharing in the Spirit, if any tenderness and compassion, then make my joy complete by being like-minded, having the same love, being one in spirit and of one mind.

Philippians 2:1–2

The apostle Paul certainly could have been tempted to think there wasn't a plan in place—or at least not a good one. He was writing from a prison and was obviously looking at his situation from every possible angle. Yet he sought God every step of the way. We would be wise to keep that focus.

I am not one for conflict—don't like it, never have, and not sure I ever will. But conflict is a part of life; it's here to stay.

Conflict can be constructive and wonderful if we are working toward a goal of resolution and change. But conflict can be damaging and painful if we are just spinning the wheels of conflict for conflict's sake.

Recently, some girlfriends met to discuss some things. What I didn't know going in to our lunch gathering was that the meeting was about me and some concerns they had. Ugh! I felt blindsided. I hadn't planned on crying that day, but I did. If up to me, the meeting never would have happened the way it did. But it did, and God used it for good—in the end. I couldn't see a plan in the pain at the time. But looking back, I see the pain, every bit of it, as God's good plan for getting me to a different place in my life, a place where I could have a breakthrough.

It's that meantime, once again, where we don't see why and we can't see how things will work for good. It's in the meantime where we lose our cool and say and do things we can't take back! Paul talks about these kinds of times:

> Whatever happens, conduct yourselves in a manner worthy of the gospel of Christ.
>
> Philippians 1:27

Do you know about good form? My friend Beth pointed out that in the movie *Hook*, every time they did something wrong, they called it "bad form." Now as a ministry team, we use the terminology good form and bad form.

I am pretty sure we would like to exclude certain events from the list of things that require a good response. But clearly Paul told the Philippians that whatever happened, they were to have good form.

When life strikes and I don't like where the bolt hit me, I usually want to respond with bad form. It comes naturally to respond negatively when the situation seems to warrant it. But

Paul told them, *whatever happens*, conduct yourselves with good form!

## God Has a Plan

I like to know there is a plan in place. I am not obsessive about sticking to a plan all the time, but it gives me comfort to know there is one. This also applies to my life and its challenges. If I am left to think that the meantimes are just mean and hard and have no real value, then I get utterly discouraged and feel sorry for myself. But if and when I believe that all the challenges I face have redeeming value for spiritual growth and development, I have courage to keep on keeping on. And not just courage—actual joy in the process of being conformed more into the image of Christ.

When I think of plans that don't seem to make sense, Joseph comes back to mind. God's plan was to make Joseph the ruler of Egypt, but in the meantime, he went through all kinds of crazy things to get to that end. Pastor Bob Cull calls Joseph's journey the "Ruler of Egypt School."

He says:

We see God's intention in Joseph's life—that he is ultimately going to be Ruler of Egypt and rescue the Egyptians and Israel—but he has quite a journey to get from Point A to Point B. Let's say you went to school and signed up to be Ruler of Egypt. You received your course outline and it said:

Step One: Use your gifts, get mocked and ridiculed by your family

Step Two: Obey your father, get beat up by your brothers

Step Three: Get sold into slavery, spend thirteen years as a slave

Step Four: Resist temptation, go to jail

Step Five: Use your gifts, spend an extra two years in jail

Step Six: Be Ruler of Egypt[1]

We can look at this now and know the end of the story. But when you are in the story yourself, it's easy to think that God has forgotten you or something has gone wrong. Maybe he has you mixed up with someone, or maybe he forgot his own plan!

Here are some key points about living in the meantime:

- God has his own timing—he is not on our schedule.
- God always has a plan even when we can't understand it or don't agree with it.
- God is always working, and his plan will be accomplished.
- God is not hindered by other people's bad choices that affect our life. He will use everything to get us where we need to be.
- Circumstances don't have to make sense to us; everything makes sense to God.
- And—drum roll—God is not in a hurry, we are!

Now I want you to know, brothers and sisters, that what has happened to me has actually served to advance the gospel.

Philippians 1:12

## God's Plan for Paul

Let's look at Paul's unfolding story as told in the Message:

I want to report to you, friends, that my imprisonment here has had the opposite of its intended effect. Instead of being squelched, the Message has actually prospered. All the soldiers here, and everyone else, too, found out that I'm in jail because of this Messiah. That piqued their curiosity, and now they've learned all about him. Not only that, but most of the followers of Jesus here have become far more sure of themselves in the faith than ever, speaking out fearlessly about God, about the Messiah.

It's true that some here preach Christ because with me out of the way, they think they'll step right into the spotlight. But the others do it with the best heart in the world. One group is motivated by pure love, knowing that I am here defending the Message, wanting to help. The others, now that I'm out of the picture, are merely greedy, hoping to get something out of it for themselves. Their motives are bad. They see me as their competition, and so the worse it goes for me the better—they think—for them.

So how am I to respond? I've decided that I really don't care about their motives, whether mixed, bad, or indifferent. Every time one of them opens his mouth, Christ is proclaimed, so I just cheer them on!

Philippians 1:12–18

It must have looked like there was no plan, but a little background from Acts 25:11 tells us what happened. What looked like Paul being sent out of the country to pacify the Jews turned out to be the opportunity God used to get Paul to Rome. As a Roman citizen, Paul could appeal his case to Caesar. Paul's appeal was used as an excuse to send him out of the country. Yes, Paul was sent to a Roman prison, but nevertheless, he was in Rome, somewhere Paul wanted to be to preach the Good News.

Paul was able to see all that had happened with remarkable perspective. He affirmed that what had happened wasn't bad. It was good. All the thwarting of the enemy and the evil of the people became opportunities for God to work in him. The difficulties became doors. What seemed to be adverse worked to advance the gospel.

This is how it is in our lives too. There is a plan. It might not make sense, but in the middle of the sleepless night, or the divorce settlement, or the bankruptcy that you never dreamed you would file for, God is working, God is shaping you, God is committed to you. His timing will culminate in his faithfulness.

**In my meantime place, I am learning . . .**

_____

_____

_____

_____

_____

**In my meantime place, God is requiring me to . . .**

_____

_____

_____

_____

**Prayer**

*Heavenly Father, I am yours, and I thank you that you have a plan for each detail of my life. You are working, and I desire to respond by trusting you. Give me the strength to look to you, having faith that there is a plan, even when it looks like there isn't one. Amen.*

# 9

## The Meantime Shapes You

### *Trials Bring Beauty to Life*

For it is God who works in you to will and to act in order to
fulfill his good purpose.

Philippians 2:13

Mocha. I hadn't stopped to think about the color of my walls
in the routine of daily life. But there I sat, unable to sleep, fix-
ated on the mocha-colored walls at three in the morning. Tick,
tock, tick, tock—the steady rhythm of the clock was the only
sound in the middle of the night. The ticking that I normally
never hear seemed like a drill in my head, reminding me how
slowly time was passing. Would it ever be morning? And when
morning came, would I face another day of emotional pain, or
would I be motivated to get going?

Life had become a series of problems. My mind was racing
endlessly, trying to figure out how to fix the problem or fix

myself. The more I tossed and turned, the louder the clock became. Tick, tock, tick, tock. I wrapped my fluffy down pillow around my ears in an effort to deaden the noise of time—another minute, another hour. When Lord? When? Why Lord? Why?

When was the last time you tossed and turned or were hounded by an endless cycle of trying to figure out how to make life behave again? There is nothing fun about a trial, test, or hard spot—nothing.

One of the most important things to remember is that there is always a plan. In each and every situation in our life, God is working, even in the middle of an unresolved situation. And though we don't always understand how God works, he works. Sometimes the best answer to our prayers is "not now." We desperately want to be out of the fire, but often God waits, and it's in the waiting, or the meantime, that we are shaped into the image of Jesus, which is what his ultimate plan is for us anyway.

I have always liked the story of the potter's house in Jeremiah. It illustrates for us how when something is marred and not turning out the way it is supposed to, God can re-form it so that something new and right can be made in its place. Take a look with me:

> So I went down to the potter's house, and I saw him working at the wheel. But the pot he was shaping from the clay was marred in his hands; so the potter formed it into another pot, shaping it as seemed best to him.
>
> Then the word of the LORD came to me. He said, "Can I not do with you, Israel, as this potter does?" declares the LORD. "Like clay in the hand of the potter, so are you in my hand, Israel."
>
> Jeremiah 18:3–6

Take note of one important thing here: the clay and all that it would become were in the potter's hands! Does it hurt when we have to be brought down so that a new and improved person can be formed? Yes! Is that breaking still God's plan? Yes. Momentary pain and discomfort give way to a greater work of shaping our life and mind into the image of Christ. And that is why we can rejoice in the middle of the shaping process. The truth is that God is working, and though some situations hurt and seem unfair, they will pass and we will be better for them, *if* we yield to him in the process.

> In all this you greatly rejoice, though now for a little while you may have had to suffer grief in all kinds of trials. These have come so that the proven genuineness of your faith—of greater worth than gold, which perishes even though refined by fire—may result in praise, glory, and honor when Jesus Christ is revealed.
>
> 1 Peter 1:6–7

## The Refining Fire of Hard Times

The beauty of God being at work in human lives is that when we turn to him, he uses our trials to refine us. The trial works on the rough edges of pride, judgment, insecurity, fear, and self-focus. And then we are thrust into the middle, or the fire of it, to be refined even further. In the middle, the dross is removed. But the flame is hot, and the removal can be painful.

God doesn't use the furnace to burn us and leave us singed and unusable. Rather, he uses the flames of our trials to make us more beautiful and usable. Now that I've depressed you with the truth about the furnace being a necessary tool at different times in life, are you ready for a wow verse? The apostle Paul left a nugget that is very encouraging and proves to be life changing.

> For it is God who works in you to will and to act in order to fulfill his good purpose.
>
> Philippians 2:13

87

Eugene Peterson in the Message says it like this:

Be energetic in your life of salvation, reverent and sensitive before God. That energy is God's energy, an energy deep within you, God himself willing and working at what will give him the most pleasure.

What gives him the most pleasure? To shape us into his image (Rom. 8:29) and to teach us to live by faith (Heb. 11:6). Both require us to be changed from the inside out and polished up.

## God Is at Work

A few years back, God made this verse real and alive to me. I am amazed to think that God himself is with me, working in me, in the middle of all my circumstances. It's easy to fall prey to the trap of only seeing God and his goodness when life is good and not believing and hoping that God is working when life is difficult. It almost seems impossible to believe that God is working despite my shortcomings and sometimes even because of them. But it is true. God is working, and in this I find comfort.

Let's break it down:

God is working in us in two areas:

1. our will: he is rearranging our mind and desires to bring us to his purpose.
2. our actions: once our mind begins to change, we start desiring different outcomes. We start acting in ways that line up with his desire.

When Paul told the Philippians that God was at work, he used *energeo*, which is the Greek word that means to be operative, to be at work, to put forth power, to work to be our aid, to effect, or to display one's activity. This is the same Greek word used in Ephesians 1:11: "In him we were also chosen, having been predestined according to the plan of him who works out everything in conformity with the purpose of his will." Just as God is working out everything to conform to his purpose and will, he is at work in our individual human lives—in our broken places, messed-up problems, and dysfunctional ways of getting by. And to that I want to shout, "Amen!"

Why is God operative in our lives? Simply because life is all about him and his plan. He has a good purpose that he desires to see fulfilled. As hard as it is to get the truth through our heads, this life is not about us. We are taught from the time we are young to make our plans and dream our dreams, but often in doing so we forget the fact that God is at work to shape us and cause us to want to walk on his good path for our life. Henry Blackaby in *Experiencing God* tells us to find out where God is working and join him. Paul said in Ephesians 2:10, "For we are God's handiwork, created in Christ Jesus to do good works, which God prepared in advance for us to do."

God is working "to will." This means he has a desire for us, the purpose, the thing that will bring him pleasure, and he is moving in us to make that happen. I like to think of it as something starting in my head—my thoughts. Many times a thought has dropped like a bomb in my brain, an idea I never would have thought of, and it makes its way into a new desire to do something different, something that moves me to fulfill God's plan. I don't realize at the time that it is God working at the level of my will so that I will act in accordance with his plan, but that is exactly what is happening.

When you became a Christian, God made you a new creation (2 Cor. 5:17). And it is God's plan to continually build new things in your life as you walk with him. Sometimes this walk with him is far from optimal due to present circumstances or sufferings. But even in these hard times, God can shape us as we make ourselves available to him and his way. He doesn't force the changes on us. Instead, he asks us to yield our will and our desires to him and to follow him rather than setting our own course for life.

How are we going to do the things he created us for? God himself is going to work in our mind—to will. He is going to give us the grace and strength, life experience and gifting to do his will. I used to ignore all my random thoughts. But now I pay attention when something persists in my head. Why? Because God may very well be trying to speak to me—to will in me—so that I will do his will.

For instance, there are times—in the middle of the furnace— when we don't want to forgive someone. We close the book on the relationship and go on our merry way, trying to avoid that person the best we can. Then we begin getting this thought: *I should let go of this hurt*. We ignore it. Our pride and flesh fight it, but it will not go away. Could it be that God is working in us to create a desire and a willingness to forgive? It amazes me how this works. He intervenes, not leaving us to figure it all out. He is working, so we should trust his work and find comfort in the truth that he calls us his own and that he has a plan for his own. It might not look like much of a plan today, but there is a plan.

We are his work! We are his people! Paul knew this when he wrote to the Philippians, and that is why he was so adamant about teaching them the truth about real life, real trial, real suffering, and, yes, real peace, hope, and joy.

> But you are a chosen people, a royal priesthood, a holy nation, God's special possession.
>
> 1 Peter 2:9

The process toward maturity in Christ involves remembering the truth. Other times we are to "do" or walk out some actions because of the truth. Both are important, for remembering plants truth deep within us and doing keeps our walk with Christ and our faith in him alive and fresh.

**In my meantime place, I am learning . . .**

_____

_____

_____

_____

**In my meantime place, God is requiring me to . . .**

_____

_____

_____

_____

### Prayer

_Lord, I am amazed that you are always active and working in my life. You are behind the scenes in the good and in the bad, working out your will and plan. You are moving me, instructing me, refining me. Help me now to follow hard after you and your ways for me rather than creating my own plans and purposes. In your name, amen._

# 10

## God Will Provide for Your Needs

### *Choose to Trust*

Do everything without grumbling or arguing, so that you may become blameless and pure, "children of God without fault in a warped and crooked generation." Then you will shine among them like stars in the sky.

Philippians 2:14–15

The excitement was building around our house. This would be the second wedding in less than three months, and we were down to the final days. Things were going just as planned, but then little issues began to pop up all around us. The weather report predicted rain on the day we were planning an outdoor wedding and reception, and if that were not enough, there were more unexpected challenges ahead—with only three days left to go.

My friend Bettina was on her four-hour drive up Highway 5 to give her gift of floral arranging for the grand event. I was home getting the guest room ready and waiting for the floral delivery truck to arrive. Excitement was in my heart and in the air.

Unlike most deliveries, the flowers came earlier than we expected. Large white boxes filled our kitchen as the delivery people brought them in one by one out of the refrigerated delivery truck. After I signed the receipt and the white truck pulled away from the house, I stood looking at those boxes, wanting to tear into them to see the beautiful fall flowers we had ordered. Orange calla lilies—from New Zealand—would be the mainstay for the arrangements.

The boxes were filled with other flowers too—terra-cotta roses, pincushion proteas, white ranunculus, and a pop of green with the belles of Ireland. All would be gathered together in the next two days to create the arrangements that our daughter had envisioned for her special day. Since I don't know much about flowers, I decided I would wait until my florist friend arrived before getting my fingers into things.

After about an hour, those boxes were calling me, really they were, and I could wait no longer. So I opened just one to peek inside. Slowly and carefully I moved the packing material aside, and to my surprise I saw an odd color peeking back at me. The flowers looked like calla lilies, but they were definitely not orange or anything resembling orange. They looked a bit like a bruised and browned banana, a far cry from the color we had ordered for a wedding that was going to have orange pumpkins down the aisle, little pumpkins on the tables, and bridesmaids decked out in chocolate brown dresses that were to be complemented by the orange of the lilies. Not only were these lilies not orange, but they were also not pretty. I had never in my life seen such a color.

Something was terribly wrong. I could hardly wait for my friend to arrive so I could see what she would do with this situation. Surely there must be a way to get new orange flowers at the San Francisco flower mart, so I was not going to worry. It would work out.

The first phase of this meantime experience involved waiting. Every time I pictured those ugly flowers I got a twist in my stomach, and each time I remembered how much those brown flowers cost—another twist. There was nothing I could do but wait for Bettina to arrive. In the meantime, I had to stay calm.

Soon my friend pulled up to the house, excited about making creations that would bless our daughter and make a lasting impression, just like the flowers she had just done for our son's wedding a few months earlier. But the look on her face told the story. The flowers were wrong, and after the bride took a sad, solemn peek, we sprang into action to find replacement orange flowers. Never mind that these ugly calla lilies cost a good part of the budget. We had to make things work. We were on a mission.

The supplier had ordered from New Zealand, and the correct color had been ordered. However, due to the weather in New Zealand, the colors can vary, so there was no return and no refund. My friend Bettina knew how to handle everyone's disappointment. "I choose to trust!" she said—and she meant it.

Trust? That was easy for her to say. After all, she wasn't the parent of the bride, one who wanted to make sure the day was everything our girl hoped it would be. I thought we'd better *do* something and quick. So I kept excusing my stress, and she kept telling me, "I am going to trust God with this. Somehow it's going to be okay."

In the meantime, we all had a choice—sit down and cry, which would only make things worse, or get busy looking for alternatives while we prayed for God to direct us. I admit that I worried and Bettina prayed while looking for alternatives.

## Our Problems Are Never Fun

The meantime is never convenient. It usually involves something that causes anxiety or concern and can tempt us to throw our joy out the window and forget the very truths of Scripture, the truths Paul was trying to teach the church.

God is faithful—whether it's flowers for a wedding, a bill that needs to be paid, a relationship that is in need of healing, an illness that needs God's touch, an emotional wound that needs the triage of God's Spirit. In the end, we will see God's faithfulness.

It's while we wait it out that it gets a little tricky and often a little messy. We can lose perspective, focus, and start living in a negative place. I think it's great to have friends who say, "I choose to trust," though I admit that can be annoying in the moment. In the end, God will provide all we need, so trusting is the right choice in the meantime.

Paul wrote to the Philippian church, telling them to do everything without all the familiar complaints we have grown to think are acceptable. He reminded them that their lives were meant to shine like stars, holding out hope in Christ. When we choose to trust, the light goes on, and we do begin to shine in our dark situations. As I slowly began to follow my friend's lead, let go of my mother-of-the-bride's worry, and turn my attention to seeing just how God was going to work, I was filled with unspeakable joy and expectation. It started with a choice, just like Bettina stated. I too had to choose to trust God with the situation.

How did God supply our need? Have you ever heard of painted flowers? I hadn't, but after a few phone calls, my friend was advised to paint the calla lilies—never mind the mess and the time involved or the fact that we could not find floral paint anywhere. Instead, we bought three cans of different colors of spray paint, prayed, and then tried it out on just one lily. After it didn't die, we figured it could work. By the end of the day, the lilies were a beautiful orange, the arrangements were done, we hadn't spent a bunch of extra money, and those painted calla lilies spoke faith to me each time I looked at them.

What started out as a wedding emergency turned into a beautiful example of how God truly knows our need and supplies what we need, reminding us that we do not have to worry and can choose to trust. Going through that day was an exercise and learning experience in my walk of faith. I saw firsthand how easily I can turn to doubt and complaining. My faith in God's power to work out even practical details was stretched and shaped. I didn't like the situation at the moment, but I grew from it.

What about you? What are your "lilies" today? What is your current emergency? Will you choose to trust?

Though we often stress and worry, it's a waste of our energy and peace. In the end, our God will show himself faithful—time and time again. It's the meantime that counts. What will you choose?

## Contentment in the Meantime

Paul gave his friends in Philippi the secret, if you will, for contentment in the meantime. Trouble is, when it comes to biblical principles, even Christians are skeptical.

We all know about the verse "I can do all things through him who gives me strength" (Phil. 4:13). We try to claim the strength verse without seeing the context. The strength Paul refers to has everything to do with contentment, and contentment has everything to do with the steps that Paul laid out like a map in the preceding verses.

Here's a recap of what he taught:

Action—there are some things we need to do
Rejoice always in the Lord!
Do not be anxious about anything.
Pray about everything.

Pray with detail and specific petitions.

Pray with thankfulness and expectancy.

Why? The Lord is near.

Promise—God's peace will settle on you

Then he goes on to say:

> I rejoiced greatly in the Lord that at last you renewed your concern for me. Indeed, you were concerned, but you had no opportunity to show it. I am not saying this because I am in need, for I have learned to be content whatever the circumstances. I know what it is to be in need, and I know what it is to have plenty. I have learned the secret of being content in any and every situation, whether well fed or hungry, whether living in plenty or in want. I can do all this through him who gives me strength.
>
> Philippians 4:10–13

Could it be that the secret to our peace and contentment in Christ is summed up in the letter to the Philippians? I encourage you to linger in the pages of Philippians, learn some of the verses, and try living in them. You'll experience God changing you—day by day. Yes, he does supply all that we need!

The next time you are tempted to doubt and stress out, try something different. Do not worry. Instead, pray and give all the details of your concern to God. Pause now to remember he is near, he is with you.

We passed the test of the flowers, but then the morning of the wedding we were told we had to tent the area because it was going to rain. What normally would have been a stressful situation was handled pretty calmly. Our daughter, the bride, took a breath and trusted God. I was amazed at her response and followed her lead. The day turned out beautifully, with the soft sound of rain on the tent and the pastor asking everyone to close their eyes and listen to the sound of their wedding day.

It had been a three-day, faith-test whirlwind, but we had learned something. We could trust God with all that concerns us. The wedding turned out more beautiful than we could have planned ourselves. The reception was moved indoors, the ceremony was tented, and the flowers were painted—and in the end, all of those things spoke volumes to us about God's true provision of all we need and more than our hearts could hope for.

My friend Bettina refused to worry about the ugly flowers. Why? She knew God would come through and supply the need. She set her mind on the truth, and her actions followed.

Because of a wrong mind-set, many people never experience the joy of living.

Joyce Meyer[1]

If God gives such attention to the appearance of wildflowers— most of which are never even seen—don't you think he'll attend to you, take pride in you, do his best for you? What I'm trying to do here is to get you to relax, to not be so preoccupied with *getting*, so you can respond to God's *giving*. People who don't know God and the way he works fuss over these things, but you know both God and how he works. Steep your life in God-reality, God-initiative, God-provisions. Don't worry about missing out. You'll find all your everyday human concerns will be met.

Matthew 6:30–33 Message

Our world is hungry for genuinely changed people. Let us be among those who believe that the inner transformation of our lives is a goal worthy of our best effort. . . . Detachment is not enough; we must move on to God—attachment. The detachment from the confusion all around us is in order to have a richer attachment to God.

Richard Foster[2]

**In my meantime place, I am learning . . .**

_____

_____

_____

_____

_____

**In my meantime place, God is requiring me to . . .**

_____

_____

_____

_____

_____

### Prayer

_Faithful heavenly Father, forgive me for not trusting you consistently. You prove yourself faithful and continue to supply all I need—and more. Teach me to learn to line up in faith the practical pieces of my life and days. And remind me to focus, remembering the lilies and the truth of your faithfulness. In your name, amen._

# 11

## Keep Your Spiritual Focus

### *God Teaches You through the Difficulties of Life*

Further, my brothers and sisters, rejoice in the Lord! It is no trouble for me to write the same things to you again, and it is a safeguard for you.

Philippians 3:1

The coffee spilled on the newly upholstered chair, your toddler smeared food all over the freshly painted wall, your husband is being difficult, your friends are not there when you need them— and you stepped on the scale to five extra pounds! Look up? Handle it spiritually? Yeah, right!

Then we go to Bible study and try to cram the truth into us, making it relate to our toddler-smearing, five-extra-pounds kind of day—and we are not sure how to make that happen or what daily spiritual focus looks like this side of heaven.

## An Upward Focus

The apostle Paul's life makes our life look pretty good. And yet he maintained a focus that kept him sane and spiritual. He encouraged others to keep rejoicing no matter what they were going through and to conduct their lives and actions in a way that would be different from the norm. What made Paul different?

Paul was characterized by a moment-by-moment surrender and an upward focus. For him to live really was Christ, and that made life different. His focus was upward. He speaks of that upward perspective, fixing our gaze in a certain direction, over and over again.

Living with spiritual focus means going about our day, doing the things of the day, and pulling our focus back to the Lord many times in the process.

- Lord, it's only a chair. Help me with my frustration.
- Lord, be with my husband and help me to be patient right now.
- Lord, you know I don't have time to clean this wall. Stretch my time so I can handle this mess.
- Lord, I am disappointed with my friends. I look to you. I commit this to you.
- Lord, I know that carbs pack on the pounds for me. Give me the self-control to pull back and get this weight off.

The things surrounding you are real, but when you look at them you are immediately overwhelmed and unable to recognize Jesus.

Oswald Chambers[1]

Only when we look up and refocus our heart and mind on Jesus can we have the attitude we see Paul teach and display:

Whatever happens, conduct yourselves in a manner worthy of the gospel of Christ. Then, whether I come and see you or only hear about you in my absence, I will know that you stand firm in one Spirit, striving together as one for the faith of the gospel without being frightened in any way by those who oppose you.

Philippians 1:27–28

The Message says:

Meanwhile, live in such a way that you are a credit to the Message of Christ. Let nothing in your conduct hang on whether I come or not. Your conduct must be the same whether I show up to see things for myself or hear of it from a distance. Stand united, singular in vision.

Philippians 1:27

Note that is doesn't say, "When life is good, conduct yourselves." Or, "When people treat you right, conduct yourselves." The message is clear. Whatever happens, we are to conduct ourselves a certain way. We are to behave or act in a certain way. And that way is the way worthy of the gospel of Christ. This is one of the key steps to living well in our meantime places.

## Whatever Happens

Conduct is from the Greek *politeuomai*, which means to fulfill one's duty, to lead one's life. Its root is in the Greek *politeuma*, which is "citizenship." Paul will later remind us that our citizenship is in heaven (Phil. 3:20). Look at what he writes in Ephesians 2:19–22:

Consequently, you are no longer foreigners and strangers, but fellow citizens with God's people and also members of his household, built on the foundation of the apostles and prophets, with

103

Christ Jesus himself as the chief cornerstone. In him the whole building is joined together and rises to become a holy temple in the Lord. And in him you are being built together to become a dwelling in which God lives by his Spirit.

Let's break this down. Whatever happens—add your thing to this—we are to lead our life as a citizen of God's kingdom. The Word tells us that we are no longer merely citizens of the world or the community we live in; we are citizens of God's kingdom. We are not foreigners in God's kingdom but foreigners in this world and this culture's customary way of handling life. This is why we can trust and rejoice in the middle of things that are not going our way. Like Paul, we can believe that God is really working in our life in all things.

So whatever happens, we are to lead our life as a woman belonging to God, fulfilling her duty as a citizen of heaven. In simple terms, I think this is saying, "Whatever happens, live up! Live up in truth, live up in response, live up in faith, live up by refusing to let this thing that has happened define you, defeat you, or derail you."

Whatever happens, we are to behave in a way that is worthy of the gospel of Christ; whatever happens, we are to behave in a way that lines up with the truth in the gospel. We cannot behave a certain way if our mind is directed otherwise. If we are looking down, self-focused, we cannot conduct ourselves in a way that honors God, because we will be living out the day in self. This is why focus and focused living are so important.

When you are tempted to lose focus, remember these four points:

1. Life can be difficult.
2. God is working through the difficulties for greater good in us.
3. Behave accordingly. Look up, trusting God no matter what the current circumstances are.

4. Live up by choosing to believe your life is under the promises of God's faithfulness, rather than living discouraged and under your problems.

When I wrote about this subject on my blog awhile back, many women posted their stories in response. Those stories paint a picture of life that is not perfect and has many "whatever happens" moments and circumstances.

- a time of wilderness and barren life
- health problems resulting in a hysterectomy and a surgical menopause that is making the sufferer feel she is going crazy
- a child that is doing all the wrong things
- upsetting news about a pregnancy with problems
- depression
- problems with church members
- a neighborhood misunderstanding
- a custody battle
- feelings of worthlessness due to a broken marriage
- secret addiction to antianxiety drugs
- needing rehab due to addiction to pain medications that no one realizes she is taking

In the midst of what you're facing today, let these two words, *whatever happens*, speak truth to you about your life, your attitude, and your current circumstances.

We also glory in our sufferings, because we know that suffering produces perseverance; perseverance, character; and character, hope. And hope does not put us to shame, because God's love has been poured out into our hearts through the Holy Spirit, who has been given to us.

Romans 5:3–5

105

Remember, do not worry. Instead, pray, giving all your concerns to God. Easier said than done, right? Stop and think about the outcome you would like. Do you want peace? If you do, then you will have to learn to stop all forms of worry in their tracks. When we worry, there is a complete absence of peace. But when we pray and surrender ourselves to God, we experience peace and centeredness on Christ.

In his book *Celebration of Discipline*, Richard Foster speaks of moving past superficial living and braving the depths of living as spiritual people. This newness comes in many forms, and a calling aside to prayer is one specific subject, or discipline, addressed in the book. I find I often get discouraged with praying because I want the answer on my own time line rather than learning to trust that prayers are heard and answered in God's timing.

Foster says:

> To understand that the work of prayer involves a learning process saves us from arrogantly dismissing it as false or unreal. If we turn on our television set and it does not work, we do not declare that there are no such things as electronic frequencies in the air or on the cable. We assume something is wrong, something we can find and correct. We check the plug, switch, circuitry until we discover what is blocking the flow of this mysterious energy that transmits pictures. It is the same with prayer. . . . We listen, make the necessary adjustments, and try again. We can know that our prayers are being answered as surely as we can know that the television set is working.[2]

### The Bigger Picture

I have had to learn spiritual focus. To do so, I came up with a reminder. I began drawing my mind's attention to a picture on the front of a puzzle box. That image reminds me to focus on the bigger picture at hand. With that picture in my mind's eye, I exhale and realize a few key things:

- It is possible to be in the middle of a problem even though I am seeking God.

- It is possible to be affected by others' poor choices and have to deal with my reaction.

- It is possible to receive a no or not now when praying and have to keep praying for God's will.

- It is possible for everything to change in one day or one moment.

- It is possible to live above the circumstances rather than under them.

- It is possible to have a new view of things and for that view to change my reaction to life.

Paul spoke of this new view as a sign of growing spiritual maturity:

> Not that I have already obtained all this, or have already arrived at my goal, but I press on to take hold of that for which Christ Jesus took hold of me. Brothers and sisters, I do not consider myself yet to have taken hold of it. But one thing I do: Forgetting what is behind and straining toward what is ahead, I press on toward the goal to win the prize for which God has called me heavenward in Christ Jesus. All of us, then, who are mature should take such a view of things.
>
> Philippians 3:12–15

Paul never claimed to have his act together. What he did claim to be was a man who sought God and a man who wanted to know Christ in all things. He also tells us that we can have a different perspective or view of things when we look for what is ahead, look up and strain toward the goal of knowing Christ.

For me, that is where the puzzle picture comes into play. When I think of it, I am reminded that every piece in the box has a place and a purpose and only the creator of the puzzle knows the finished picture. For me, my God, my Creator, knows the finished picture of my life and how the current piece fits into it. So in the meantime, I choose to pray and trust instead of worry. How about you?

**In my meantime place, I am learning . . .**

_____

_____

_____

_____

_____

**In my meantime place, God is requiring me to . . .**

_____

_____

_____

_____

### Prayer

_Lord, teach me to look to you in the moment of things happening in my life. And may I develop the attitude that whatever happens I will live to conduct myself in a manner pleasing to you. Teach me how to rejoice in my meantimes, how to choose you over my spinning and stressing. I need a teacher because it does not come naturally to me. Please pour your Holy Spirit fresh on me, as I am in this waiting place, and teach me to honor you with my days. Amen._

# 12

## Resist Fear by Relying on God

### *Trust His Mighty Grip*

We who serve God by his Spirit, who boast in Christ Jesus, and who put no confidence in the flesh.

Philippians 3:3

I wish I could send the Lord a text message today. I need immediate response to my inner turmoil. Each hour that passes makes my stomach twist a little more. And what's a girl to do when she is upset? Either eat or obsess over her Facebook page!

We are so tied to social networking—Twitter, Facebook, blogs, and email—that I feel like God himself should message me back, and quickly. But that's not the way it works.

Paul didn't send emails, but he did write letters to encourage others. He took his pain and his momentary troubles and wrote letters to help guide the way for others who needed guidance. He wrote things like, "What has happened to me will turn out for my deliverance. . . . I eagerly expect and hope that I will

. . . have sufficient courage. . . . For to me, to live is Christ. . . . Whatever happens, conduct yourselves in a manner worthy of the gospel. . . without being frightened in any way by those who oppose you" (Phil. 1:19–21, 27–28).

Sometimes people oppose us. Paul knew that kind of opposition. But what about when Satan himself is opposing you? Remember, we don't just fight against people but against powers of wickedness in high places. Even when a situation has a tangible person or event attached to it, don't forget that there is a spiritual battle going on. And Satan wants to use anything and everything to get you to take your eyes off Jesus and take part in some pretty ungodly conduct.

The thing that Satan uses the most to take us down is fear. Fear is the opposite of operating in the healing balm of love. "Perfect love expels all fear" (1 John 4:18 NLT).

Some of us aren't as afraid of the boogeyman as we are of people. We worry when a friend or associate hurts us. Rejection is a very hard pill to swallow, and it is solidly rooted in fear. And if it's not people we are afraid of, maybe it's our things, or our future. Yes, focusing on the "what ifs" in life can stir up much fear in our hearts—keeping us right where Satan wants us—too troubled and tormented for our own good.

### Sometimes We Have to Get a Grip

My friend's boyfriend dumped her. She wasn't expecting it, and the pain was unbearable. After a few sleepless nights, tossing and turning in fits of tears, she knew she had to get a grip—she just didn't know how.

We all know the pain of breakups, hurts, unfair accusations, relational problems, financial difficulties, and the like. Life is hard. We read we are not to sweat the small stuff, but really, even the small stuff looms large at times, doesn't it? Since we cannot change the small stuff or the large stuff (if we could, we wouldn't be in a turmoil about it), it's important that we understand how to live in the spaces of life where there is emotional pain.

Because of God's love for us, bad things are turned to good things. Does this mean that everything is a blessing? No. I have experienced many bad things that remained bad in themselves. But those very things were used in my life to shape me, form me, change me, and make me the woman God had always designed for me to be. And this type of change is always a good thing.

Seeing this theme played out in Scripture helps us make it a part of our own lives today. Let's look at what Paul says:

> Yes, and I will continue to rejoice, for I know that through your prayers and God's provision of the Spirit of Jesus Christ what has happened to me will turn out for my deliverance. I eagerly expect and hope that I will in no way be ashamed, but will have sufficient courage.
>
> Philippians 1:18–20

> So how am I to respond? I've decided that I really don't care about their motives, whether mixed, bad, or indifferent. . . . And I'm going to keep that celebration going because I know how it's going to turn out. Through your faithful prayers and the generous response of the Spirit of Jesus Christ, everything he wants to do in and through me will be done. I can hardly wait to continue on my course. I don't expect to be embarrassed in the least.
>
> Philippians 1:18–20 Message

There was a lot of turmoil in Paul's life when he wrote this. His enemies were taking advantage of his chains and trying to cause trouble with their selfish preaching. His friends were worried that he might die. But Paul continued to look up. He looked to God. He set his heart to live under the promises rather than under the problems of his day.

He looked up, and in doing so, he knew that in all things Christ would be glorified in his life.

What was his attitude toward those who were unfairly using him or those who hurt him? So what? Those preaching to gain advantage of his imprisonment were at least preaching the message. Those praying? At least they were praying. And the threat of death? No problem. Paul knew whether in life or in death he belonged to God and would be with him forever. This guy had unshakeable peace.

## Trust God

A while back I had some turmoil in my life that seemed unjust and unfair. I could not believe God would allow it to happen. I can remember praying something like, "Lord, you know I already have rejection issues, so why would you allow this to take place?" And the answer I heard was straight from Philippians. What is happening to you will turn out for your deliverance. Immediately, the purpose behind the pain made sense to me. I didn't like the trial, but I wanted more and more freedom from past hurts and from operating in my flesh—in any way, shape, or form. So I began to see these pressing places of pain as God's wonderful tool in my personal life.

What about you? Where are you today? Have you been hurt? Do you feel things are unfair? Do you suppose that God can use this pain to bring you to a better place? I don't know when your meantime will end, but I do know it will. Everything we go through is ultimately temporary!

> For our light and momentary troubles are achieving for us an eternal glory that far outweighs them all. So we fix our eyes not on what is seen, but on what is unseen, since what is seen is temporary, but what is unseen is eternal.
>
> 2 Corinthians 4:17–18

If everything is ultimately temporary, then in our meantime, we are especially to ask him for the strength to walk in the truth and to practice the things we see in God's Word. The best thing for us to do in difficult situations is to stop putting our trust in self or other people and put our trust in God alone.

> Put no confidence in the flesh, but put your confidence in God.
>
> Philippians 3:3 (author's paraphrase)

Here is one of my favorite passages:

> Trust in the LORD with all your heart
>     and lean not on your own understanding;
> in all your ways submit to him,
>     and he will make your paths straight.
>
> Proverbs 3:5–6

I memorized it years ago but only experienced it when I began to endeavor to live it out in my own life. I did that by picking it apart and realizing there was a pattern to follow each day:

- Make a decision each day to trust God.
- Refuse to lean into my own reasonings, manipulations, or ideas.
- Turn over each situation to be solved to God.
- Acknowledge that he has the ultimate solutions to all of my life needs.
- Trust and claim the truth that God is in the process of making the map of my life by making my paths straight.

I have a plaque in the master bathroom of my house, where I see it every morning. It reads:

> Lord, help me to remember that nothing is going to happen to me today that you and I cannot handle together.

113

**In my meantime place, I am learning . . .**

_____

_____

_____

_____

_____

**In my meantime place, God is requiring me to . . .**

_____

_____

_____

_____

_____

### Prayer

*Jesus, thank you for being my deliverer, my healer, and the one who lifts my head. I trust you to make good of bad and to use all things to bring me into more spiritual health and freedom. May I, like Paul, have the attitude of, So what? My God is with me! Amen.*

# 13

## Live with Courage

### *Anyone Can Fall Apart; Be Different*

But whatever were gains to me I now consider loss for the sake of Christ. What is more, I consider everything a loss because of the surpassing worth of knowing Christ Jesus my Lord, for whose sake I have lost all things. I consider them garbage, that I may gain Christ and be found in him.

Philippians 3:7–9

It felt like a slap in the face, though I wasn't physically touched. Cutting words, cruel and attacking my intentions and my character, stung and left me immobilized for several days. Looking back, I guess you could say I was slapped in the heart—where it hurts the most.

Have you ever been slapped in the heart? Perhaps a loved one has treated you cruelly, or a friend has turned her back on you, or you are not getting along with the people you work with or live by. Relational drama is where the rubber really meets the road in our lives. It is easy to have peace when things are going well, but take an emotional hit from someone you love, and things can go downhill fast.

Women frequently tell me that the pain of feeling misunderstood and judged is more than their little people-pleasing hearts can bear—and boy do I understand! I deeply respected the person who was using pointed words, ugly sneers, and a raised voice, which made the slap to the heart sting even more. Exiting the building as quickly as I could, I ran for cover in my car. I cried my heart out and feared the worst. Nobody likes to be misunderstood or judged, but it's part of life. Falling apart seemed out of my control at the time, as every reserve in me was crying long before I shed a single tear.

Life happened to me that afternoon, and it changed me. At first the change was terrible—fear, anxiety, emotional upheaval. Later, change took the form of posttraumatic stress episodes every time I saw the person. Eventually, change came in the form of peace and a settled heart toward the offender and a willingness to see the situation and everyone else who has ever hurt me through different eyes. What started as fear was turned over and changed by God's love.

## Have Courage

When life happens and situations are not going our way, we can easily find ourselves deeply entrenched in places of fear, insecurity, and doubt. In the heat of our emotional response to things, we often find ourselves reacting in ways that have to be retracted later.

The apostle Paul was no different. He was human. He battled with the human condition, the desire for significance, and all the things we struggle with. His personal challenges may differ from mine, and mine may differ from yours, but the struggle of life continues today—in people like you and me.

> Part of you is numb; the other part, frantic. You detest feeling fragile, and you dislike being needy. But you're coming apart at the seams. This is not how you planned your life.
>
> Kari West[1]

Paul encouraged the Christ followers to have a "whatever happens" attitude. Whatever happens, we are to live as citizens of a new kingdom, conduct ourselves in a new way, and live up to what God has called us to as his people. This way of living is not a life of perfection but rather a life of position. We take our position and stand as his people in our real-life battles.

Second Chronicles 20 contains the story of King Jehoshaphat, who was alarmed when he found out an army was coming against him. As we read the account of his response, we find that he turned to God when he didn't know what to do. His eyes were on God for direction, strength, and help. And God responded to this humble surrender:

> This is what the LORD says to you, "Do not be afraid or discouraged because of this vast army. For the battle is not yours, but God's. . . . You will not have to fight this battle. Take up your positions; stand firm and see the deliverance the LORD will give you. . . . Do not be afraid; do not be discouraged. Go out to face them tomorrow, and the LORD will be with you."
>
> 2 Chronicles 20:15, 17

Paul is teaching the spiritual practice of taking your position by telling his readers, whatever happens, conduct yourselves differently. In Ephesians, Paul stated it this way: "As a prisoner for the Lord, then, I urge you to live a life worthy of the calling you have received" (4:1).

Live a life worthy of the calling—no matter what happens. In the meantime, learn to live differently than just settling for living according to our moods, attitudes, or fears.

Paul says in Philippians 1:28, "Without being frightened in any way by those who oppose you." In a trial of any kind, something is opposing us. The opposition can come from people or circumstances. Sometimes we feel as though life itself is opposing us.

It is the same today as it was when Paul wrote this letter. Our culture may be different from his, but the human condition is not. Our trials may be different—people were not going through short sales and bankruptcy—but Paul's readers had their own problems. Scripture is relevant today, and we need to understand that it takes courage to walk with Christ—in the meantimes of life.

- It takes courage not to sink down into fear or insecurity but to stand in our position as his child.
- It takes courage to trust God when unsaved family and friends think it is a bit radical or irresponsible to trust God with our problems.
- It takes courage to conduct ourselves in a way people are not accustomed to us acting.
- It takes courage to choose faith and upward focus rather than fear and defeating depression.
- It takes courage to go to the Lord with our problems instead of fussing and fretting about them over a latte with friends.

Let's build on what Paul is teaching us. Whatever happens, in the meantime:

- Conduct yourself in a manner worthy of the gospel. Live like a citizen of heaven, like you are truly his.

- Resist being frightened in any way by those who oppose you. When life or people oppose you, trust the God who holds your life.

## Run to God

I am excited about things the Lord is pressing into my own heart. I have spent some aha time with Jesus. I just walked through one of the worst seasons of my life and can now see how God used it to shape me. I was opposed in many areas. I was hurt and fearful. But God, in his goodness, used this time for furthering me in my walk with him. The opposition changed me, drew me to Jesus, and caused me to grow. Remember that Paul said, "What has happened to me will turn out for my deliverance" (Phil. 1:19). Perhaps what is happening to you is going to be the thing that sets you free or plants you in a better place—after you have walked through the meantime of it.

So whatever happens, throw your arms in the air right now and say, "Whatever!" Not a haughty or cynical whatever but a joyful, abandoned, courageous whatever!

And what about the fear? If you are fearful today, remember that God loves you, and sit with the truth of his love. Why love?

> There is no fear in love. But perfect love drives out fear, because fear has to do with punishment. The one who fears is not made perfect in love.
>
> 1 John 4:18

The answer to fear and anxiety lies in what we believe, not what we say we believe. If we believe in God's love for us and that we belong to him, we will walk through the meantimes with our head a little higher and our heart a little lighter.

What do you fear today?

- your circumstance?
- the disapproval of people?
- financial collapse?
- loss of health?
- a marriage that is not what you dreamed?
- a child who is not living as you wished?

Live with courage. How? By running back to God, over and over, resisting fear and the enemy who lies to us at every turn.

> Humble yourselves, therefore, under God's mighty hand, that he may lift you up in due time. Cast all your anxiety on him because he cares for you. Be alert and of sober mind. Your enemy the devil prowls around like a roaring lion looking for someone to devour. Resist him, standing firm in the faith, because you know that the family of believers throughout the world is undergoing the same kind of sufferings.
>
> 1 Peter 5:6–9

Let's review the steps because we need a plan in our meantime places—a place where it is easy to forget God is with us in whatever happens.

- Have faith that this problem can be a positive growth experience.
- Ask for courage to live one day at a time.
- Whatever happens, watch your life and conduct.
- Walk in obedience and surrender.
- Resist complaining and look past yourself.
- Put no confidence in the flesh, but put your confidence in God.

In my meantime place, I am learning . . .

_____

_____

_____

_____

In my meantime place, God is requiring me to . . .

_____

_____

_____

_____

### Prayer

_Dear Lord, I am good at being afraid, turning my heart and mind toward the what ifs, and not very good at rejoicing in the whatevers. I need more security in your love, care, and concern for me. Train me in love, build me up in the most holy faith, and in my current situation keep me humbly coming to you for help and hope. Amen._

# 14

## Consider Others

*Learn to Live beyond Yourself*

I want to know Christ—yes, to know the power of his resurrection and participation in his sufferings, becoming like him in his death, and so, somehow, attaining to the resurrection from the dead. Not that I have already obtained all this, or have already arrived at my goal, but I press on to take hold of that for which Christ Jesus took hold of me.

Philippians 3:10–12

While we wait for things to get better, for life to fall into place, or for grief to subside a bit, it's important not to be completely self-focused. Paul writes from his meantime, giving the Philippian church spiritual insight and practices for successfully living the life Christ has called them to. Each practice is important any time, but being spiritually focused and directed is especially important during the meantime places, when life can seem mean and days are too long. Paul's desire to press on to know Christ despite his troubles is our example today.

When I am going through difficulty, I feel the world should stop too—take note, give me a break, lend me a hand, or at the very least care. But often we go through our meantime places alone. Sure, friends might know we are going through something, but they can't be with us 24/7. One thing is certain: if we sit around waiting for everything to get better, we will end up waiting alone in our own sadness and negativity.

A woman emailed me that she was about to have the wrong attitude on her daughter's birthday because of her own pain. "It's one of my kids' birthdays today, and it's been a surgical menopause type of day since I woke up. I couldn't shake the sadness that I felt in my heart knowing I was grouchy and it would affect her on her birthday. Then I remembered God gives me a second chance when I forget about myself. So I ordered pizza for her class today to celebrate, and by the time the little class pizza celebration was over, I was out of my sour attitude. How terrible it would have been had I missed showing my daughter love on her birthday."

Paul, in the first chapter of Philippians, states his condition (in chains), proclaims the promise of a purpose in suffering (it will turn out for my deliverance), and affirms his mission statement (to live is Christ). He spends the rest of the letter, like a good coach, showing the believers in Philippi how to live in real life. Interestingly, he begins with how they should live toward one another. So whether you are single, married, widowed, or divorced, you need to learn how to live with others in a way that honors Christ. You and I don't get a pass for being hormonal, cranky, or insensitive. We don't get a pass just because we are in a meantime place in life.

Paul tells the Philippians:

> If you have any encouragement from being united with Christ, if any comfort from his love, if any common sharing in the Spirit,

if any tenderness and compassion, then make my joy complete by being like-minded, having the same love, being one in spirit and of one mind. Do nothing out of selfish ambition or vain conceit. Rather, in humility value others above yourselves, not looking to your own interests but each of you to the interests of the others.

Philippians 2:1–4

The Message says:

If you've gotten anything at all out of following Christ, if his love has made any difference in your life, if being in a community of the Spirit means anything to you, if you have a heart, if you care—then do me a favor: Agree with each other, love each other, be deep-spirited friends. Don't push your way to the front; don't sweet-talk your way to the top. Put yourself aside, and help others get ahead. Don't be obsessed with getting your own advantage. Forget yourselves long enough to lend a helping hand.

Philippians 2:1–4

Paul gives some practical advice for living. He starts with how we should treat others. This is not surprising, since Jesus himself taught that the two most important kingdom principles were to love him and love others. It all sounds poetic and beautiful, but in real life, if we get our buttons pushed, watch out! Or what about when we are having a bad day? What if someone else gets promoted? What if a friend gets the guy and we don't? And what if she is more talented, prettier, and has a better way of connecting with others? What if just being around her makes us feel "less than"? And what if her life looks easy and ours is painfully hard?

It's a funny thing, but it's true: when you reach out and give to others, when you sow into others' lives, when you love when you don't have it in you, God blesses you far more than you can imagine. Jesus himself lays out this principle in Luke 6:38: "Give, and it will be given to you. A good measure, pressed down, shaken together and running over, will be poured into your lap. For with the measure you use, it will be measured to you."

When life is hard and it seems like you can't make it through another day, put into practice the instruction in the first four power-packed verses in the second chapter of Philippians. If there is any love in you, share it with others. If there is any life left in you, consider others and their needs. If you are in a hard place, give your interests to God and look out for others who are in a hard place too.

The culture we live in does not follow this plan. I am supposed to look out for numero uno—me. But Paul is teaching us, as a good coach, that if we have received anything from Christ, we should show it by how we live in regard to others. These points are worth remembering: see ourselves with humility, consider others in a Christ-centered way, look out for the welfare of others.

> When you come to personal dealings with others, remember who you are—You are not some special being created in heaven, but a sinner saved by grace.
>
> Oswald Chambers[1]

How do I consider others? Have my inner barriers gone up toward others? Am I looking for reasons not to get along? Am I easily intimidated? Does this keep me stuck in my stuff, unable to reach out for help and unable to reach out to others?

Paul teaches us to make our life about Christ and others. He was in jail and could have wallowed in self-pity and self-focus, but in his meantime place, he reached out to others—encouraging them to put Christ first, live in humility, and always consider other people.

Has your pride (stubbornness or anger, insecurity or self-pity) kept you from thinking of others and living in the truth of Christ's teaching during your difficult season? It's time to think about what Scripture says and reach out in love, even if it's a baby step. Reach out to others and put yourself aside. You will find that it is actually good medicine for your own pain.

Kari West reminds us:

> From time to time everyone encounters frustration and despair. The apostle Paul did. After his conversion on the road to Damascus, he encountered incredible obstacles. He lost his possessions and comforts and he faced unpopularity and incarceration, but he didn't give up, give in, or give way to hopelessness. There were probably moments when Paul doubted his progress just as we do. . . . When we realize that the daily battle is the Lord's, we can confront the boulders that are in our way. Ask yourself: What am I going to do about this? Do I cry or slam my fist on the table? Go crazy? Quit my job? Pack up the computer? Adopt out the kids? Or do I finish the course, believing I am really going to be okay?[2]

Today take a step that will get you outside of self long enough to think of someone else.

> A generous person will prosper;
>    whoever refreshes others will be refreshed.
>                                    Proverbs 11:25

**In my meantime place, I am learning . . .**

_____

_____

_____

_____

_____

**In my meantime place, God is requiring me to . . .**

_____

_____

_____

_____

_____

### Prayer

*Jesus, I come to you today wanting to humble myself before you. I am sorry that I get self-focused and act like I am the only one who has problems. Help me to see past myself, help me to live in truth, help me to consider others and in doing so to honor you. I want to learn how to give extravagantly even when I am hurting, even when my schedule is full and I have nothing in myself to give. In these times, show me, Jesus, how to live outside myself and how to put myself aside. Amen.*

# 15

## Live Loved

### *No Thing Separates You from God's Love*

I press on toward the goal to win the prize for which God has called me heavenward in Christ Jesus. All of us, then, who are mature should take such a view of things.

Philippians 3:14–15

The setting was perfect—on a bluff above a golf course, with lush green hills and carpets of white roses. There was just enough sun to warm the guests and just enough wind to create a soft breeze. The bride was stunning. The groom's anticipation as she made her way down the rose-covered aisle was priceless. Love was in the air the day my son and his wife took their vows—for better or worse, till death do us part.

They were committing to love each other and stay true, even in the meantime places of life, when there doesn't seem to be a solution to life's problems.

When we know we are loved, the problems, though there, don't seem to overwhelm us. We take them on—one day at a time, one moment at a time. But when we get distracted and absorbed in self, the problems loom larger than we can handle. We begin to stir in our angst and focus on "poor me."

When we know we are loved, we walk through difficult times with the knowledge that we are supported and cared for. We know that someone else walks with us. The meantime places are not as harsh or lonely when we do not walk through them alone.

The same is true for us on our journey of faith. Whether married, single, divorced, or widowed, we never walk alone. It might look like there is only one set of footprints, but there are always two.

## God's Love

Often we forget that God is with us, and we live like the world is on our shoulders. Our problems take on a life of their own. We feel frustrated with the mounting pressures and realize we are incapable of handling all that is coming our way. That is why, especially in the hard times, it is important to live a lover's life—walking hand in hand with God, embracing his presence with us, and holding on to his promise to love us through eternity.

> Who shall separate us from the love of Christ? Shall trouble or hardship or persecution or famine or nakedness or danger or sword? . . . No, in all these things we are more than conquerors through him who loved us. For I am convinced that neither death nor life, neither angels nor demons, neither the present nor the future, nor any powers, neither height nor depth, nor anything else in all creation, will be able to separate us from the love of God that is in Christ Jesus our Lord.
>
> Romans 8:35, 37–39

Your present circumstance may be pulling you under, and you may very well feel separated from God's love. In the moment, you may know you are separated from the love of others, and that hurts. But in reality, at the end of the day, there is *no thing* that can separate you from the loving hand of God. Not illness, divorce, distress, or death of a loved one. Not financial loss, relational stress, or unfair treatment by others. Life hurts, but God heals the hurt, using everything to bring us to a place that is grander than where we started. God loves us, cares for us, and redeems us from the hand of the enemy—friend, foe, or principalities and powers. No thing can separate us from the love of Christ Jesus our Lord.

In the New Testament, we are called the bride of Christ. He has made his intentions toward us obvious. He is committed to standing by us through thick and thin, for better or worse. He is with us today and in every meantime place from here to eternity. Paul wanted the church to live in this love—to live a lover's life. Lovers are committed to each other. They overlook faults and believe in the best. Lovers have optimism because they believe that the love they have can see them through the tough times ahead. We too can live a lover's life in relation to Jesus Christ.

How does this love message translate to our real problems? Understanding the love of God in experience gives us confidence while in the middle of our problems. For instance, today is wet and soggy in California. I have a bad cold that started a few days ago, and all I feel like doing is staying under the covers. It's dry under the covers, and my throbbing head could get some relief. But the truth is, it's just a cold. I have had colds before, and I have full confidence that it will be better soon.

Confidence comes from experience. Our experiences of God being with us in the past can give us confidence for the present and the future.

## Paul's Prayer

Though Paul had his own problems—like being in jail—he thought of others, prayed for them, and longed to see them have better lives in Christ.

> And this is my prayer: that your love may abound more and more in knowledge and depth of insight, so that you may be able to discern what is best and may be pure and blameless for the day of Christ, filled with the fruit of righteousness that comes through Jesus Christ—to the glory and praise of God.
>
> Philippians 1:9–11

> My prayer for you is that you may have still more love—a love that is full of knowledge and wise insight. I want you to be able always to recognize the highest and the best, and to live sincere and blameless lives until the day of Jesus Christ. I want to see your lives full of true goodness, produced by the power that Jesus Christ gives you to the glory and praise of God.
>
> Philippians 1:9–11 Phillips

> So this is my prayer: that your love will flourish and that you will not only love much but well. Learn to love appropriately. You need to use your head and test your feelings so that your love is sincere and intelligent, not sentimental gush. Live a lover's life, circumspect and exemplary, a life Jesus will be proud of: bountiful in fruits from the soul, making Jesus Christ attractive to all, getting everyone involved in the glory and praise of God.
>
> Philippians 1:9–11 Message

Paul knew that God was always at work in human lives. He banked on it, believed it, and prayed accordingly. After reminding the Philippians that God would complete the work he had begun in them, he also commits to pray for them in some specific areas:

- love—love much and well
- knowledge—that brings every wise insight
- discernment—to recognize the highest and the best
- sincere and blameless lives—faith not sentiment
- fruitfulness—lives full of true goodness
- glorifying God—lives that bring him praise through thick and thin

Love is not flimsy. It is not a pat on the back, a smile, or just a nice word. Love has meat to it, a stick-to-the-ribs quality. For love to abound, the other firm attributes must follow close behind. And this is what Paul prayed for his friends.

I like that Paul gives us examples of what he prayed, examples that translate into real life. So today I am going to think about the list, making sure that the five things that come after love are important to me as well.

God is at work in our lives, and love is the main thing that will glorify him, give us strength to stand, and give us faith to believe. And like all things worth having, love must be developed, and development happens as we are tested. When life is hard and relationships sour, it is not easy to love. But it is in the hard place that we are tested, tried, and developed to gain the kind of love Paul is praying for here.

Where are you today? Remember that the testing of your faith is producing something wonderful that you cannot yet see. The testing of your faith might come in the package of relational drama or personal turmoil. Think of what Paul prayed (as paraphrased by me) and pray this for yourself when you hit hard times.

- love much and well
- use your head
- test your feelings

- live in faith not sentiment
- pray for bountiful fruits of the soul
- live a life that makes Christ attractive to all

Dear friends, let us love one another, for love comes from God. Everyone who loves has been born of God and knows God. Whoever does not love does not know God, because God is love. This is how God showed his love among us: He sent his one and only Son into the world that we might live through him. This is love: not that we loved God, but that he loved us and sent his Son as an atoning sacrifice for our sins. Dear friends, since God so loved us, we also ought to love one another.

1 John 4:7–11

Paul prayed that the Philippians would be filled with love. Being filled with love is to be filled with God himself. Today I am praying to be filled with God himself, for in the meantime, being filled with God himself will help me go the distance. It is not flimsy faith or fluffy words but the infilling of God's Spirit in my very heart. Join me in praying for the heart of God as you walk through life in the meantime.

Consider it pure joy, my brothers and sisters, whenever you face trials of many kinds, because you know that the testing of your faith develops perseverance. Let perseverance finish its work so that you may be mature and complete, not lacking anything.

James 1:2–4

If you were to live loved in your current situation, how would you live differently through your situation? I see a picture of a woman who is beginning to trust God from a place of being loved by him. Remember, there is no fear in love. God is love (1 John 4).

**In my meantime place, I am learning . . .**

_____

_____

_____

_____

_____

**In my meantime place, God is requiring me to . . .**

_____

_____

_____

_____

_____

### Prayer

_Lord, I want to thank you for loving me. It is difficult to comprehend the love that your Word speaks of. It is not the conditional love that I have known in this life. I am asking you to fill me with this unconditional love that I might quit being stingy with human love, being able to experience the supernatural love of God for myself and for others. In this love I put my confidence today and declare in praise that no thing can separate me from you and your care. Amen._

# 16

## Practice Obedience
## One Step at a Time

*Life Can Be Ugly, but God's Ways Are Beautiful*

Therefore . . . you whom I love and long for, my joy and crown,
stand firm in the Lord in this way, dear friends!

Philippians 4:1

Life was hitting a good friend hard. Her husband was becoming increasingly difficult, and her anger and frustration were
mounting by the day. There was no end in sight to their problem
because they were deadlocked in a disagreement and neither one
of them cared to give in. With both wanting to be right, no one
was going to win. She was stuck in a meantime, but she played
a part in what was keeping her there. Often meantimes are like
that. It's easy to point the finger at someone else, but when we
recognize our role in the difficulty, we realize that God may
expect something of us too. My mother used to tell me, if you

point a finger at someone else, just be aware that three fingers are pointing back at you.

Meantimes often revolve around relationships. When misunderstandings turn ugly, a lot of damage can be done. Attitudes are left unchecked, and confidence in God and his way of doing things seems to get discarded.

In every meantime situation, whether it be marital, friendship related, work related, health or finance related, there is something that God is calling us to—and that something is a simple act of obedience that may not feel so simple at the time. What God is requiring of me will be different from what he is asking of you. And for each of us, obedience will be different in each situation. One thing is certain: obedience has much to do with our attitude, and Paul gave some spiritual direction on that as well.

To his friends in Philippi, he wrote:

> Therefore, my dear friends, as you have always obeyed—not only in my presence, but now much more in my absence—continue to work out your salvation with fear and trembling.
>
> Philippians 2:12

God calls us to walk out our salvation—to live in it, move with it, not just use it as a fire insurance policy!

## Why We Don't Want to Obey

Recently, God made it clear to me that my attitude toward a certain situation in my life had to change. What had been done was clearly wrong, but my bad attitude was not going to get me anywhere, and it certainly was not going to make things better. I was not carrying around the same attitude as Jesus. I was not making my self nothing but instead was making my feelings everything. I was going to have to be obedient to a death of self-interest and pride. I didn't want to be obedient. I wanted my way, my rights, my rule! Do I hear an amen? But I don't find any of those things in God's directives for living, and certainly Paul wasn't instructing the church to live a life based on self, feelings, and the confidence that our way is the right way.

*Obedience* is a word that can strike fear, angst, and rebellion in us—fear that we have to do something we don't want to do, angst because we realize we are better off obeying than not, and rebellion because we like to live on our own terms, not God's. Sometimes the word *obedience* brings out our rebellious nature, and we want to stomp and shout, "I don't have to do it if I don't want to!"

I can still remember when our oldest child turned eighteen. In our culture, there is something magical about that number. You can join the armed forces and you have a right to declare your freedom as adults. But when our son turned eighteen, he was a senior in high school. Somehow we didn't get the memo that because he was eighteen he no longer had to do things according to his parents' standards, even though he was still under our roof!

After a few little battles, we got the situation straight, but the angst he had in turning eighteen and finding he still had to obey us reminds me of the angst we often have with God, or the resistance we often have to the truth in his Word. We hold on to the verses we like while resisting the ones that are too difficult or uncomfortable. Paul tells us the importance of a life humbled before our Maker and an attitude of complete surrender to the one from whom life came. I like the way Eugene Peterson phrases this passage in the Message:

> What I'm getting at, friends, is that you should simply keep on doing what you've done from the beginning. When I was living among you, you lived in responsive obedience. Now that I'm separated from you, keep it up. Better yet, redouble your efforts. Be energetic in your life of salvation, reverent and sensitive

before God. That energy is God's energy, an energy deep within you, God himself willing and working at what will give him the most pleasure.

Philippians 2:12–13

## A Better Plan

It is an act of humility to put someone else's plan or wishes above our own. Jesus humbled himself and became obedient to death. His obedience brought pain and suffering. He knew what was coming and he obeyed anyway. He knew he was God in the form of man, yet he still went through the suffering. Why?

Because he knew there was a plan, and the plan included God sending his only Son to die for our sins. It had to be done this way. It was the sacrifice that would grant us our salvation. There is a story, a plan, and a way that things are to play out. Jesus knew this and submitted to it. He obeyed.

Paul was a living example of this same type of obedience. Jesus was the model for Paul, and he spent his ministry teaching others, encouraging them to look at life differently, react to life spiritually, and obey God more readily.

If we really believe there is a greater story working in our lives, we will obey too. We often forget that God ordained our days (Ps. 139:16). We forget that we are his work and that he already prepared good works for us to do (Eph. 2:10). We forget that he will complete, accomplish, or perfect everything that concerns our life (Ps. 138:8). I think it's time to remember.

What is the one thing you keep sensing God is asking you to obey in your current situation? What is keeping you from humbling yourself to obey?

> Give me understanding, so that I may keep your law
> and obey it with all my heart.

> Direct me in the path of your commands,
> for there I find delight.
> Turn my heart toward your statutes
> and not toward selfish gain.
> Turn my eyes away from worthless things;
> preserve my life according to your word.
>
> Psalm 119:34–37

**In my meantime place, I am learning . . .**

_____

_____

_____

_____

**In my meantime place, God is requiring me to . . .**

_____

_____

_____

_____

**Prayer**

*Heavenly Father, I come to you with my life, and today I am reaffirming that you are the maker of me, the boss of me, and have the best plan for me. I am asking you to teach me how to obey you and how to follow your ways. Help me, Lord, to look to you, to place my confidence in you, and to confidently follow you even when it is difficult and even when I am walking into territory I would rather not face. May the cry and prayer of my heart be, "Yes, Lord!" In your name, amen.*

# 17

# Do Everything without Complaining

## *You Don't Have to Be Miserable*

Finally, my brothers, rejoice in the Lord! It is no trouble for me to write the same thing to you again.

Philippians 3:1

When faced with a new challenge, what is your attitude? Most of us have a life theme. What is yours? Did you know that rejoicing can become your life theme?

I am not happy to have to admit that worrying and complaining—or as my mother used to say, "a dog chewing on a bone"—was my normal default behavior, even as a Christian. I had to challenge this behavior in me, and I still have to give myself checkups and tune-ups on this one. Every time I think of being critical or complaining, it helps me to remember this verse:

"Do everything without complaining or arguing, so that you may become blameless and pure, children of God without fault in a crooked and depraved generation" (Phil 2:14–15).

We can gloss over our bad attitudes and words all we want, but the truth comes out of us. What is on the inside is what trickles out through passive-aggressive actions or snotty, insensitive words. We often trick ourselves into believing we are just noticing or caring about a negative for prayer purposes. But, the dictionary says to complain is to express feelings of dissatisfaction, pain, or resentment. The synonyms here are gripe, kick, bellyache, whine. Now—is that clearer?

I think for many of us, the normal pattern is to gripe and whine about what our feelings are at that moment. What would happen if we went about our lives without complaining or kicking at every single thing? Perhaps to become a woman that trusts God, we need to develop a new pattern and new habits in the meantime.

Most of us have a pattern that we live by when we are faced with problems. Sometimes we complain and make everyone around us miserable. It's easy to lose focus and allow our minds to go from A to Z, from bad to worse, and from faith to fear. The thing that amazes me the most about Paul is his focus on Christ's faithfulness in the middle of his problems. He trusted without a solution in sight! He was confident, and that confidence in the midst of trial or suffering was attractive. Paul's God confidence brought honor to Christ.

But he wasn't the only one. Throughout Scripture, we see many men and women who trusted God despite hardship. Let's look again at King Jehoshaphat, for instance.

### An Example of Trust

The king of Judah, Jehoshaphat, was busy raising up leaders in the land when he found out that a vast army was coming against him and his people. When I first read this story, I was relieved that even strong kings get alarmed when trouble comes. But there is much to be learned from his story and how he handled the problem. Let's just say he didn't know what to do! Brilliant. This is someone I can relate to.

Life was going along, he was responsibly doing his duties, and overnight he was hit with an enemy attack. Can you relate? You are living life as usual and bam! For Jehoshaphat, the meantime began the day he heard that the army was plotting. I learned something about dealing with my meantime places by paying attention to the first few things he did when crisis hit:

Alarmed, Jehoshaphat resolved to inquire of the LORD.

2 Chronicles 20:3

First things first—he was alarmed (a sudden feeling of fear). A multitude of things can bring on that sudden feeling of fear: you just found out your husband is having an affair, you lost your job, or you received a bad medical report.

We can all relate to being alarmed when we hear bad news. But in this case, despite his fear, Jehoshaphat resolved to go to God. To resolve means to "make a firm decision, to state formally in a resolution, to find a solution to, to deal with successfully."[1] How do you like that? He made a decision to deal with what was alarming him "successfully"!

Jehoshaphat was a king. He had power and authority. Yet, even powerful people in high places get scared and have their confidence shaken when life hits them upside the head. After resolving to seek the Lord's help, he proclaimed a fast and held a meeting. He stood in front of the people and began:

LORD, the God of our ancestors, are you not the God who is in heaven? You rule over all the kingdoms of the nations. Power and might are in your hand.

2 Chronicles 20:6

And he concluded:

For we have no power to face this vast army that is attacking us.
We do not know what to do, but our eyes are on you.

2 Chronicles 20:12

Let's pay attention and learn from this. When we don't know what to do, when we are rocked by a new circumstance, when we are weak and life hits us hard, leaving us alarmed, afraid, and stressed-out, the first thing we need to do is put our confidence, trust, and the situation in God's hands.

I know firsthand that it is easier to complain to a friend, go on a carbohydrate binge, or indulge in some other source of personal comfort. But the thing that will make a difference is to quit talking about trusting God and resolve to really do it!

Our sense of confidence is fickle at best. We feel strong when things are going our way and when we have a handle on things. But throw us a curve ball and our sense of confidence is shaken. We plummet into worry, fear, and anxiety. We complain or wallow in self-pity. We try as fast as we can to cover up the areas that we are having trouble holding together.

It's interesting that in this place of weakness, in our mean-times, God can do his finest work in us. It is in the meantimes that we can learn amazing spiritual principles. Jehoshaphat was about to learn a few things. God's response to the humbled king was this: "This is what the LORD says to you. 'Do not be afraid or discouraged because of this vast army. For the battle is not yours, but God's'" (2 Chron. 20:15).

To recap:

- Jehoshaphat got some bad news, and he was afraid.
- He turned to God and admitted he did not have what it took for this battle.
- He put his eyes on God for help.

- God told him, "Don't sweat it, King J. The battle is mine. Don't be afraid."

We'll get to the end of this story later. For now, let's return to Philippians and Paul.

## Properly Placed Confidence

How did Paul tell his friends to live life?

> For to me, to live is Christ. . . . Whatever happens, conduct yourselves in a manner worthy of the gospel of Christ . . . without being frightened in any way by those who oppose you.
>
> Philippians 1:21, 27–28

> Therefore, my dear friends, as you have always obeyed—not only in my presence, but now much more in my absence—continue to work out your salvation with fear and trembling, for it is God who works in you to will and to act in order to fulfill his good purpose.
>
> Philippians 2:12–13

> I press on to take hold of that for which Christ Jesus took hold of me. . . . One thing I do: Forgetting what is behind and straining toward what is ahead, I press on toward the goal.
>
> Philippians 3:12–14

> Rejoice in the Lord always.
>
> Philippians 4:4

Think of your current hard place. Now go through the steps of the example given to us in the story of Jehoshaphat, adding the words of Paul as an instruction in how we are to conduct ourselves in trouble. As long as you and I trust in ourselves, we will never experience God or his power and presence in our meantime places. But when we humble ourselves and admit we don't have what it takes, he meets us in that place and speaks comfort and promise to our heart.

Paul learned the secret of contentment and the value of properly placed confidence. He didn't learn them in a nicely furnished Bible study classroom but in a prison cell. It appears that even in desperate situations, contentment and properly placed confidence go hand in hand.

When our confidence is properly placed, our life is like one big stress-relieving exhale. We stand taller, we breathe deeply, we trust fully. We believe God is faithful and we can trust him.

Do we still fear? Yes, but our fears no longer have to torment us. We have our big-girl faith pants on. We can live in God confidence, pure and simple. Well, maybe not so simple.

There is no pat answer because the meantime is different in every situation. Sometimes the meantime feels like it will last forever. And, yes, often the meantime appears to be mean, unfair, unjust, unfamiliar, unreal. In the meantime places, we need to learn how to cope, how to live, and how to move forward—without complaining.

Here's an example of some meantime places:

- You are single and have prayed for God to bring a man into your life, but in the meantime, you are alone every Saturday night.
- Your marriage is a mess. Your husband is not interested in making it work, and you can't do it on your own. You are praying for your marriage to be healed, but in the meantime, it hurts to be sleeping in separate beds.
- You lost your job and are having trouble finding a new one. You can't survive on unemployment. You have to move, and everything is up in the air. You know you will

eventually land on your feet, but in the meantime, you are frustrated, scared you won't find another job, and are moving into your parents' guest room.

- You decided it's time to start a family. You are excited about the dream of being a parent, but in the meantime, you have trouble getting pregnant, and each month is a disappointment.

- You have just had your first baby—what a joy! But you are not doing well with the new schedule and no sleep. Even though it feels like forever, you know it's not, but in the meantime, you have to figure out how to handle your new life.

- You have twenty dollars left in your checking account, and payday isn't for five days. In the meantime, you have to make it on four dollars a day.

- Your teenage daughter is on drugs. You put her in a treatment program, but in the meantime, you wait and pray for her to be clean and sober again.

I think you get the picture.

Back to King Jehoshaphat—he could have complained, grumbled, kicked everyone around him, and griped his head off. He could have also taken things into his own manipulative hands, but instead he turned to God and did not complain, but listened for God's instructions to stand firm and to send worshipers out in front of the army. We see the result of the King's obedience and the way praising God works as the story ends with . . .

As they began to sing and praise, the LORD set ambushes against the men of Ammon and Moab and Mount Seir who were invading Judah, and they were defeated.

2 Chronicles 20:22

> And the kingdom of Jehoshaphat was at peace, for his God had given him rest on every side.
>
> 2 Chronicles 20:30

Have you been complaining too much in the meantime? Have you been taking your frustration out on other people? What would it look like if you trusted God, stopped the whining, and began to praise God? The army King Jehoshaphat sent out sang, " Give thanks to the LORD, for his love endures forever" (2 Chron. 20:21).

Now let me ask you, can you make "his love endures forever" your song of praise, by faith?

> Jesus Christ knows our circumstances better than we do, and He says we must not think about these things to the point where they become the primary concern of our life. Whenever there are competing concerns in your life, be sure you always put your relationship to God first.
>
> Oswald Chambers[2]

**In my meantime place, I am learning . . .**

_____

_____

_____

_____

**In my meantime place, God is requiring me to . . .**

_____

_____

_____

_____

**Prayer**

*Lord, help me to see things as they are, not how they feel. You are with me always and through everything. Help me to keep looking up to you and living in the truth in your Word. Give me a teachable heart while I am in the frustrating and uncomfortable meantime places in life. Amen.*

# 18

## Rejoice in the Lord

### Practice the Rejoice Choice

But in every situation, by prayer and petition, with thanksgiving, present your requests to God.

Philippians 4:4-5

I have spent most of my adult life in church ministry. Part of my job includes pastoral care, and I have spent time in hospitals, by bedsides, and visiting people in their last days. Usually I expect to find people who are hurting, a little grumpy about their situation, or pretty needy. And in each situation, I understand why they are not themselves. I have watched my parents at the end of their lives and many other people over the years, and it's clear that it is much harder emotionally and mentally than I can imagine. Those of us in a meantime that we know will end someday can look ahead, but often those who are in a meantime that will end in death have trouble seeing the unknown, even if they have professed faith all their lives.

So that is what I expected when I visited a woman from our church at her house after she was diagnosed with terminal cancer. To my surprise, that visit turned out much different than I had expected.

She greeted me at the door dressed in a darling leisure outfit, hair perfectly done and makeup beautifully placed on her aging face. After thanking me for coming, she showed me to the sofa in her living room, where we sat and began to visit. She told me about her diagnosis of end-stage cancer, which was not found on earlier tests, and professed her trust that God always knew it was there. She told me she was at peace. Then all at once she got a little twinkle in her eye and asked her husband to get something from the other room. In a minute or two, he came back carrying a little case, which he placed on the table before us. Opening her little treasure chest, she smiled as she showed me all the beautiful hankies she had collected over the years. Some were embroidered, others were painted, and some were exquisite prints of fabric. She had such joy as she showed me her collection and even more as she invited me to take one.

"Pick one out to remember me," she said with a smile. Feeling a little awkward, I chose a flowered print hanky and sat looking at it a little stunned. After all, here I was visiting her to comfort her, and instead she was comforting me. Yes, she knew she had cancer and was not having any more treatments. Yes, she knew she was dying. But even in her current situation, one that would make most people self-focused, she was thinking of others. She was looking for the good. She was appreciating all she had experienced in life, and that included her friendships. We were new acquaintances, and so she told me about her family and some of her amazing friends. Her love for her daughter and her granddaughter was touching. The way she chose to be thankful rather than bitter left me walking to my car with a tear-stained face.

I will never forget that day or the beauty in her face, the twinkle in her eye, and the hanky I took from her little case. How I thank God for her deposit into my life that day, her example of trust, of looking for good beyond her own circumstances.

This woman could have been bitter—the doctor had missed the cancer—but she chose differently. For days I kept thinking that if she could turn her heart around to praise despite her circumstances, so could I—and so could everyone. She reminded me that day of something the apostle Paul was trying to teach the church. It's okay to rejoice in life—even imperfect life. Rejoicing is a safeguard, a safety latch on our mental health, our emotional stability, and our relational health.

Judith could have been grumpy and sad, and anyone would expect that and feel bad for her. But she was glad in the Lord because he was good, even though her circumstances were not. She was shining that day like a star. She was holding on to the life she had left while hoping for the life she would have after her body died.

I never heard one complaint in the two hours we visited, but I did hear a lot of gratefulness for God's faithfulness throughout her life. She was a clear example of someone rejoicing in the Lord, even when any of us would have excused her if she didn't. But that day, in the moment, she was living out the secret of contentment and the main thrust of what Paul was trying to teach the Philippians.

Paul didn't say we should not feel sad or grieve, but he did encourage us to hope in God in the midst of anything that causes sadness or grief in this life. In any situation, we can practice looking for the good and make it a discipline to rejoice in the goodness of God.

Do everything without grumbling or arguing, so that you may become blameless and pure, "children of God without fault in a warped and crooked generation." Then you will shine among them like stars in the sky as you hold firmly to the word of life. And then I will be able to boast on the day of Christ that I did not run or labor in vain.

Philippians 2:14–16

Paul goes on to say:

Further, my brothers and sisters, rejoice in the Lord! It is no trouble for me to write the same things to you again, and it is a safeguard for you.

Philippians 3:1

How are you handling your meantime? Have you been complaining about every aspect and arguing with others out of frustration? If you have, I hope you'll be encouraged today to look to God and begin to be grateful, yes, even thankful, while in the meantime place. The situation doesn't have to be good for us to remember that God is good and to thank him for who he is!

Finally, . . . whatever is true, whatever is noble, whatever is right, whatever is pure, whatever is lovely, whatever is admirable—if anything is excellent or praiseworthy—think about such things.

Philippians 4:8

A saint realizes that it is God who engineers his circumstances; consequently there are no complaints, only unrestrained surrender to Jesus.

Oswald Chambers[1]

**In my meantime place, I am learning . . .**

_____

_____

_____

_____

_____

**In my meantime place, God is requiring me to . . .**

_____

_____

_____

_____

_____

### Prayer

_Lord, help me to feel and then deal when I am in a meantime situation. You are not surprised by my grief or disappointment, so help me to deal with both in every meantime by believing and hoping in your goodness. I want to develop a habit of rejoicing in you. Thank you for making it clear that rejoicing in you and putting my confidence in you keep me safe mentally, emotionally, and spiritually. So, Father, may the rejoicing begin! Amen._

# 19

## Put Your Confidence in God

### Confidence in the Flesh Is a Dead End

Whatever you have learned or received or heard from me, or seen in me—put it into practice. And the God of peace will be with you.

Philippians 4:9

Cassie is a smart woman. She is a physician and makes decisions all day long that impact her patients. People trust her, her education, her wisdom, and her experience. It's easy to see why Cassie has learned to put the majority of her trust in herself and just a small percentage of her trust in God. Her trust life is kind of like tithing: God gets 10 percent, and she takes care of the rest. It works for her—or so she thought.

Cassie's personal world fell apart, and none of her educational wisdom prepared her for waiting out the storm. She came up with an action plan, and when it didn't work, she felt fear and angst.

But she's a smart one, so she came up with another plan and tried it until it too failed. Before long she was completely at her wits' end. Do you get what I am saying here? At *her* wits' and wisdom's end. Then finally God could show himself smarter, stronger, and more faithful than she ever gave him credit for in the past.

Paul speaks of this too:

> Watch out for those dogs, those evildoers, those mutilators of the flesh. For it is we who are the circumcision, we who serve God by his Spirit, who boast in Christ Jesus, and who put no confidence in the flesh—though I myself have reasons for such confidence.
>
> If someone else thinks they have reasons to put confidence in the flesh, I have more: circumcised on the eighth day, of the people of Israel, of the tribe of Benjamin, a Hebrew of Hebrews; in regard to the law, a Pharisee; as for zeal, persecuting the church; as for righteousness based on law, faultless.
>
> But whatever were gains to me I now consider loss for the sake of Christ. What is more, I consider everything a loss because of the surpassing worth of knowing Christ Jesus my Lord, for whose sake I have lost all things.
>
> Philippians 3:2–8

In the third chapter of Philippians, Paul warns that Christians get too wrapped up in earthly things and get distracted from trust in Christ. To illustrate, he describes why he has reason to place confidence in the flesh but that in the end those things are not enough.

You see, Paul was religious before he was saved, but religion could not save Paul. And though he had the best possible reputation as a rabbi and training that surpassed that of his friends, they were not enough for real life change. Only Jesus Christ and faith in Christ could do the real job, the inner work, and the miracle that each of us needs. So he instructed others to stop placing confidence in themselves, in the ways of the flesh, in the education or pedigree that makes up their background, and instead to get to know Christ and his power in their circumstances.

This applies so well to women like Cassie who have much going on in terms of educational background or financial stability. Though our background may benefit us in many ways, when it comes to spiritual life, it sometimes gets in the way because we gravitate toward trusting in self and our wisdom instead of going to Christ for his wisdom and his work in a situation.

What is your situation? Where are you placing your confidence today? What is confidence?

- Confidence: Reliance or trust, a trusting relationship, belief and faith.

Why do we need to live with properly placed God confidence?

- Putting our trust in God brings about strength and peace. It is God's best for us.
- Putting our confidence in God brings about the abundance that all of us want in our lives. Putting our confidence in the Lord causes us to grow and flourish.
- Putting our confidence in God honors him and pleases him.

How do we do this? What does Scripture teach us?

In him and through faith in him we may approach God with freedom and confidence.

Ephesians 3:12

Let us then approach God's throne of grace with confidence, so that we may receive mercy and find grace to help us in our time of need.

Hebrews 4:16

> This is the confidence we have in approaching God: that if we ask anything according to his will, he hears us. And if we know that he hears us—whatever we ask—we know that we have what we asked of him.
>
> 1 John 5:14–15

Take your current meantime situation and go to God with it. Approach him freely and often. Find help and grace by turning to him with your need. Believe he hears you and will answer.

While you wait for the answer in the meantime:

- Turn your heart toward God.
  - The one who trusts the Lord receives blessing.
  - The one who trusts the Lord does not worry and continues to bear fruit.

- Keep returning your thoughts back to faith in God.
  - The one who does this finds that worries quiet down.
  - The one who does this finds confidence and strength.

- Stay in God's Word.
  - You can't trust without faith, and faith comes from the message of the truth found in God's Word.
  - Find verses to hold on to, to memorize, to put on cards and carry with you.
  - When tempted to doubt, refer to the truth in these verses.

- Live out your faith.
  - True faith has action steps.
  - Go about your life like one who truly believes the Lord has your problems handled and press on to learn what he wants to teach you through it all.
  - Real confidence produces hope and peace.

- Put no confidence in self-strength or self-life.
  - You can do a lot of things, but trusting self is a dead end.
  - As believers in Jesus Christ, we must learn to put our trust in his strength working in us, through us, and for us.

If we have only what we have experienced, we have nothing. But if we have the inspiration of the vision of God, we have more than we can experience. Beware of the danger of spiritual relaxation.

Oswald Chambers[1]

Back to Dr. Cassie. She tried with all her might to fix things, but others would not cooperate and the problem did not go away. Finally, she turned to God, not with a quick bless me or help me prayer but with a real laying-it-all-down prayer. When she did, he began to direct her, and as she followed, things began to change. In time, a few months of more meantime, the situation turned around, and in the end, Cassie was changed by realizing how much she depends on self more than God.

We don't have to be physicians to be like Cassie. Most of us depend on ourselves or our ideas. Maybe like Cassie we could learn a lot from trying a different approach.

> Your hands made me and formed me;
>   give me understanding to learn your commands. . . .
> May your unfailing love be my comfort,
>   according to your promise to your servant.
>
> Psalm 119:73, 76

**In my meantime place, I am learning . . .**

_____

_____

_____

_____

_____

**In my meantime place, God is requiring me to . . .**

_____

_____

_____

_____

### Prayer

_Lord, it's so easy to trust in things I have learned along the way, articles I have read, or things I have seen others try. It is not as easy to place all my confidence in you. Forgive me. Help me to realize like never before that you are not only all-knowing but also all-powerful, in each and every situation. I place my hope and confidence in you today. Continue to teach me how to do this. Amen._

# 20

## Forgive Others, Forgive Yourself, and Receive God's Forgiveness

### Experience the Freedom of God's Grace

I can do all this through him who gives me strength.

Philippians 4:13

Many of us end up in the middle of a mess due to something we have done. Perhaps we didn't intend for a situation to turn out the way it did, but even the best intentions often result in a heap of frustration and hurt. I have talked to many people over the years who are stuck in a rut because they will not forgive a wrong done to them or will not let themselves off the hook for a wrong they have done to someone. This, my friends, is a growth area for every one of us.

All of us make mistakes—not just some people, not just bad people, but all of us—you, me, the people we love most, and the people we don't like much at all. Each person is subject to the human condition, and though we try our best to do the right thing, even praying about our decisions, sometimes what we do backfires and hurts someone.

## Growing in Maturity

Anyone can spend her life defending herself and putting down others. If you want to stay in a rut, that model guarantees success. But if you want out of the pain and want to grow in the meantime of relational misunderstanding and crisis, you will need to apply the attitude and spirit Paul taught the church in Philippi.

Stop and think of your current situation. Is there a relational piece that needs to be taken seriously or given over to the Lord? As you acknowledge your personal situation before God, reflect on some of the building blocks of Philippians up to this point and apply them to your life.

- My prayer is that your love may abound more (Phil. 1:9).
- The unfairness of the situation? What does it matter? The important thing is Christ (Phil. 1:18).
- What has happened will advance you in spiritual growth and ultimately advance God's kingdom through your life touching the lives of others (Phil. 1:19).
- To live is Christ (Phil. 1:21).
- Whatever happens, conduct yourself as his (Phil. 1:27).
- Don't be afraid of those who oppose you (Phil. 1:28).
- Suffering and pain are a part of life and can change us by helping us examine what we believe (Phil. 1:29).
- Do nothing out of selfish ambition (Phil. 2:3).
- Consider others better than yourselves (Phil. 2:3).
- Christ humbled himself and became obedient; this should be our attitude (Phil. 2:5–8).
- Do everything without arguing or complaining (Phil. 2:14).

- Shine like stars in this world with the light of Christ (Phil. 2:15).
- Don't just look after your own interests but also the interests of others (Phil. 2:21).

Maturity is reflected in how we handle our situations. Do we deal with our part, feel the pain, and continue to press on toward all that God has for us?

Frankly, when I am hurting, I don't feel very mature. In fact, when I am hurting, I often stew and spin. But I am learning. I desire spiritual maturity, and I try to look at painful circumstances as a spiritual boot camp for my maturity.

Now don't get me wrong. I don't enjoy pain and the hard work of boot camp. But I do like the results of all that hard work. We can't have it both ways. Live a life based on self, and we will not show much maturity. Live a life digging into God's Word and applying what we are learning, and we will not only mature through our problems but also be changed.

What does this look like in the meantime? It is an attitude of:

- accepting the suffering
- taking responsibility for ourselves before God
- forgiving anyone who has caused or played a part in our suffering
- forgiving ourselves if we have caused the pain and suffering
- pressing on to growth while releasing the past mistakes to God

## The Process of Forgiveness

Have you made a mistake? Have you participated in a verbal sparring, a lie, a betrayal? Has this mistake landed you in your current situation? Perhaps you have checked out of life because you are discouraged or depressed and people are frustrated with you. Whatever the mistake, own it and ask God to forgive you, ask the people it has affected to forgive you, and put the mistake and the past behind you.

The first part of the process is to admit our wrong, take responsibility, and then receive God's forgiveness. That includes letting ourselves off the hook because God covered us and our mistakes with his grace. The problem with this first part is that we often get defensive, push back, or start other problems to take the attention off what we did wrong. We justify our attitude or actions because the other person did ten things wrong to our one thing. We have to stop this, look only at ourselves, and get right before God.

Forgiving ourselves is hard, especially when others try to interfere by accusing us relentlessly or holding grudges against us. But no matter what other people say, think, or do, the Word of God is clear on what happens when we own our sin, confess it, and go to Jesus. God forgives us, no ifs, ands, or buts.

Satan does not want us to believe this, so he will set up a constant stream of situations to keep us self-focused. He may turn our focus to how someone hurt us or how our mistake hurt a relationship. When this happens, we need to apply the model of Jesus when he was hungry, thirsty, and in the desert. When tempted by Satan, he used the Word of God as his defense (Matt. 4). So as we sit in our mess, tempted to think others are wrong and we are right, or tempted to think our mistake is the worst thing ever and is destroying our life, we can remember the Word of God. Jesus forgives—period. We must also forgive—period. This does not mean we will forget the offense. It simply means we will lay it aside and move on, knowing that all of us are sinners saved by grace.

Unless we receive forgiveness, it is impossible to forgive others. . . . Our worst and God's best met on a battlefield called

Calvary. God won! Jesus' victory there is God's Good News to those who will receive it.

Sandra Wilson[1]

What if the others involved don't move on quite so easily? That might be part of your suffering in this season, but you can continue to trust yourself to God.

> If we claim to be without sin, we deceive ourselves and the truth is not in us. If we confess our sins, he is faithful and just and will forgive us our sins and purify us from all unrighteousness.
>
> 1 John 1:8–9

None of us is without sin! So fess up and ask whomever you offended to forgive you. And forgive—or lay aside—the times others have hurt or wronged you. We will stay stuck in this meantime place if we do not press on and take hold of Christ in the middle of the situation at hand.

> Is anyone among you in trouble? Let them pray. . . . Confess your sins to each other and pray for each other so that you may be healed. The prayer of a righteous person is powerful and effective.
>
> James 5:13, 16

**In my meantime place, I am learning . . .**

_____

_____

_____

_____

_____

_____

**In my meantime place, God is requiring me to . . .**

_____

_____

_____

_____

_____

_____

### Prayer

*Oh Lord, I have trouble when I am accused or wronged. I have trouble not pointing the finger and even more trouble letting the offense go. And when I make a mistake, I beat myself up relentlessly and get distracted and discouraged. Worse yet is when I try to take responsibility and the other party will not forgive me or let it go. Help me in all of these kinds of meantime experiences. Help me to receive and truly embrace your love and forgiveness for myself and for others. May I press on—through tears, through hard spots—and someday reach the goal of being with you and having you say, "Well done." For this I pray, amen.*

# 21

# Watch Your Perspective

*Learn to Reframe Your Circumstances in Truth*

I have learned to be content whatever the circumstances. I know what it is to be in need, and I know what it is to have plenty. I have learned the secret of being content in any and every situation.

Philippians 4:11–12

A new woman began attending the morning Bible study I was teaching. She always carried a camera with her just in case there was a photo opportunity during her day. One week my son led worship for us, and so naturally when it was over, she took a picture of mother and son together—that day's photo opportunity. The next week she came to the study with a gift bag for me. As I opened her gift, she explained that she wasn't sure of my décor, so she gave me some options. To my surprise, I pulled three framed pictures of me and my son from the bag. It was the picture she had taken of us the week before. She had framed it three ways. I was touched by her thoughtfulness.

Later that day I took the pictures out of the gift bag and placed them on the counter in my kitchen. There was a pewter frame that said "Family" on it, a contemporary glass block frame, and a sparkly frame adorned with beautiful crystals in the same color as my house décor. Soon the phone rang, and I got busy and forgot all about those frames on the counter until my other son came over and asked why I had three pictures of me and Cameron on the counter. I explained it to him, and then we both took note of how the picture looked different based on which frame it was in.

As I thought about this later, I realized the same thing happens with our circumstances. Could this explain why people handle difficult situations differently? We each take a problem or challenge and frame it based on what we believe. How we frame things can tell us a lot about ourselves and about our need to know more of Christ's presence in the middle of each circumstance.

This is what Paul was trying to teach in the letter to the Philippians and in so many of his other letters. He frequently repeated the same principles to different groups, but the message of how to live abandoned to God was clear throughout his ministry. He also made it clear that life will include suffering and that even in the pain we can learn to press on, fix our attention on the goal, trust that Christ understands and is working, and believe with every fiber of our being that Christ conforms all things according to the purpose of his will. If and when we believe these things, we become more mature in our faith and take a different view of our life and the meantime places. We become better able to frame our circumstances with hope in God. And in that particular frame, the details of the picture appear different than they did when we framed them in hopelessness. How we view our life circumstances changes how we walk through them.

Let's sit a while in Philippians:

> But whatever were gains to me I now consider loss for the sake of Christ. What is more, I consider everything a loss because of the

surpassing worth of knowing Christ Jesus my Lord, for whose sake I have lost all things. I consider them garbage, that I may gain Christ and be found in him, not having a righteousness of my own that comes from the law, but that which is through faith in Christ—the righteousness that comes from God on the basis of faith. I want to know Christ—yes, to know the power of his resurrection and participation in his sufferings, becoming like him in his death, and so, somehow, attaining to the resurrection from the dead.

Not that I have already obtained all this, or have already arrived at my goal, but I press on to take hold of that for which Christ Jesus took hold of me. Brothers and sisters, I do not consider myself yet to have taken hold of it. But one thing I do: Forgetting what is behind and straining toward what is ahead, I press on toward the goal to win the prize for which God has called me heavenward in Christ Jesus.

All of us, then, who are mature should take such a view of things. And if on some point you think differently, that too God will make clear to you. Only let us live up to what we have already attained.

Philippians 3:7–16

Eugene Peterson, in the Message, says it like this:

So let's keep focused on that goal, those of us who want everything God has for us. If any of you have something else in mind, something less than total commitment, God will clear your blurred vision—you'll see it yet! Now that we're on the right track, let's stay on it.

Philippians 3:15–16

What is the goal in our problems? According to Paul, the high goal is knowing Christ more and more in and through everything.

Oswald Chambers also speaks of this goal:

We are not sanctified for ourselves. We are called into intimacy with the gospel, and things happen that appear to have nothing to do with us. But God is getting us into fellowship with Himself. Let Him have His way. . . . The first thing God does is get us grounded on strong reality and truth. He does this until our cares for ourselves individually have been brought into submission to His way. Why shouldn't we experience heartbreak? Through those doorways God is opening up ways of fellowship with His Son. Most of us collapse at the first grip of pain. We sit down at the door of God's purpose and enter a slow death through self-pity. . . . He comes with the grip of the pierced hand of His Son, as if to say, "Enter into fellowship with Me; arise and shine." If God can accomplish His purposes in this world through a broken heart, then why not thank Him for breaking yours?[1]

When I speak, I use those three framed pictures of my son and me to make a point. Even though the photo is the same, it has a different feel in each frame. So let me ask you, what is your current challenge? And how are you framing it?

You might be thinking, "What do you mean, how am I framing it? I didn't choose this situation, and I am not framing it at all. It came pre-framed for me, and I resent the frame!"

I understand that feeling. It took me many hard life lessons to learn that even though things come my way that I didn't choose and don't like, I am the one who gets to put them in the frame that they will sit in while they are displayed on the counter of my life. And you are the only one responsible for the framing of your circumstances too. Which frame will you choose? The sparkle of hope that God really is who he says he is, or the discouragement of hopelessness as you profess Christ but live like he really doesn't exist in your everyday details?

As a child of God you are called to be a faithful steward of your thought life. . . . You can point the spotlight of your attention wherever you like.

Tommy Newberry[2]

Let's review the things we have been learning about living in the meantime:

- Remember that when bad things happen, God is still in control and is still with you.
- Live one day at a time, one step at a time, and listen for his leading.
- Remember that God does not always explain the plan, even when you are in it. This develops your trust muscle.
- Remember that things happen *to* you so something greater can happen *in* you. Your current situation can be moving you into greater places of spiritual health and freedom.
- Praise him even when the situation is not praiseworthy, because God is always faithful to his people.
- Do not worry. Instead, pray and give all details of your concern to God.
- Be aware that sometimes the best answer to your prayers is no or not now, even when you're in an uncomfortable place.
- Practice perspective each day by looking up and believing in the bigger picture.
- Look for good and dwell on anything good while in the meantime places of life.

Therefore, my brothers and sisters, you whom I love and long for, my joy and my crown, stand firm in the Lord in this way, dear friends!

Philippians 4:1

**In my meantime place, I am learning . . .**

_____

_____

_____

_____

_____

**In my meantime place, God is requiring me to . . .**

_____

_____

_____

_____

_____

### Prayer

_Lord, I come to you now with my broken frame, asking you
to give me a new frame in which to place the details of my
life. I am asking for the frame of faith and hope. I want to
put each and every trial within the frame of Christ's care for
me, trusting that every detail of every problem will be used
to draw me to Jesus and to teach me how to have fellowship
with him at the deepest level of my being. I want to have such
a view of things. So, Lord, teach me to look to you, to long
for you, and to trust you with each framed piece of my life.
Amen._

# 22

## Say No to Anxiety

*Fretting Leads You down the Wrong Path*

Do not be anxious about anything.

Philippians 4:6

I remember it like it was yesterday, though it was several years ago. I was on the phone with someone from church who was in a messy situation. After the call was over, I sat in the chair in my backyard for quite a while, distressed by the insensitivity that people can bring to life's table and relationships.

While I was sitting with my head bowed, my son who was about ten at the time came out to the backyard to comfort me. He lifted up my chin and with a silly proud grin said, "Mom, stop fretting. 'Do not fret—it only leads to evil.'" As quickly as he appeared, he giggled and left. Do not fret? A child told me to stop fretting? How did a kid his age even know the word *fret*?

Well, that got my attention for sure. I asked God to help me quit fretting and went in to make lunch for the family. Then I saw where he got his wisdom from. His Bible verse from his Sunday school class hung on the refrigerator: "Do not fret—it only leads to evil" (Ps. 37:8). Not knowing what I was going through, he thought he would use his verse on me—and it worked!

## Why We Should Not Worry

I am now of the age when hormone levels shift and crazy things take over a woman's body, like surges of heat and feelings of panic. It's not fun, but I am learning to frame it. It has certainly been a less-than-fun meantime season, but it's a part of life, and Christ is with me in all of life. Christ giving me strength in everything is my current frame of reference!

Medical and hormonal issues create one kind of anxiety. But the kind Paul was writing about is the garden-variety anxiety commonly known as fretting and worrying. Anxiety is a state of uneasiness, worry, or fear. All of us know about anxiety.

Paul was trying to get the Christians in Philippi to grasp the truth that they have a heavenly Father who cares and takes all their concerns seriously—and has the power to work in the details of each one. With God himself at the helm, there is no need to spend our energy worrying.

Let's look at what Paul says:

> Their mind is set on earthly things. But our citizenship is in heaven. And we eagerly await a Savior from there, the Lord Jesus Christ, who, by the power that enables him to bring everything under his control, will transform our lowly bodies so that they will be like his glorious body.
>
> Therefore, my brothers and sisters, you whom I love and long for, my joy and crown, stand firm in the Lord in this way, dear friends! . . .

The Lord is near. Do not be anxious about anything, but in every situation, by prayer and petition, with thanksgiving, present your requests to God.

Philippians 3:19–21; 4:1, 5–6

It is natural for us to have our mind on earthly things while we live on planet Earth. We have responsibilities and lives to live. True. But the greater truth about us is that our citizenship is not here but elsewhere. As foreigners here, we are living here and doing business here, but we have a loyalty to our home country, the one that awaits us later. Because of this, Paul says, "Therefore . . . do not be anxious about anything." Why? Because our citizenship is in heaven, and our Lord is working in and through our lives while we live them out here on earth. He is the blessed controller of our circumstances. So why worry?

Jesus addresses worry in the Gospel of Matthew:

So do not worry, saying, "What shall we eat?" or "What shall we drink?" or "What shall we wear?" For the pagans run after all these things, and your heavenly Father knows that you need them.

6:31–32

## How to Say No to Anxiety

Where are you today? Today I am not personally worried about physical provision, but I certainly need emotional provision. Jesus would say to me, "Deb, do not worry, saying, 'When will I feel like myself again? How will I ever let these walls of hurt down? How can I trust when people keep being overly critical of me?'" And then I think the Lord would tenderly tell me, "Deb, those who do not have a God to hope in worry endlessly about what people think of them. They work hard at appearances for acceptance sake. But you know me, and you know I am working in all things, and you know I provide what you need. Therefore, do not be anxious about anything."

So the next time anxiety strikes, have a plan of action to resist it at its inception. I personally like to imagine a red stop sign being held up, reminding me to stop the thought. Then my personal plan of action looks something like this: I change my focus to what is good. I personalize Bible passages that fit my situation. They might look something like this:

- I, Debbie, have Christ in me, and in him I live and move and have my being (Acts 17:28).
- Christ is working in my situation right now to will and to do his good purpose (Phil. 2:13).
- God is my refuge and strength, a very present help in [my current trouble goes here] (Ps. 46:1).
- Christ is working in all things to bring about good and growth in me (Rom. 8:28).
- Christ is for me, so it matters not who is against me (Rom. 8:31).
- God will fulfill his purpose and all that concerns me (Ps. 138:8).
- It has been granted for me to believe and to suffer, so God will give me grace in both (Phil. 1:29).
- What is happening in my life right now will further my deliverance into freedom in Christ (Phil. 1:19).
- The Lord is Debbie Alsdorf's shepherd, and she belongs to him, and he has designed for her to live in abundance of life in him (Ps. 23:1; John 10:10).

Next, I pay attention, and each time the worry crops up, I filter it through the promises of God's Word and replace my frame on it! Finally, as I go about my day talking to others, I avoid words of doubt and fear because those conversations will only reinforce the problem. As I use words that affirm God's care over the situation, the truth of a loving God being the controller of my life and circumstances is reinforced, and anxiety flees.

Paul says:

> Rejoice in the Lord always. I will say it again: Rejoice! Let your gentleness be evident to all. The Lord is near. Do not be anxious about anything, but in every situation, by prayer and petition, with thanksgiving, present your requests to God. And the peace of God, which transcends all understanding, will guard your hearts and your minds in Christ Jesus.
>
> Finally, brothers and sisters, whatever is true, whatever is noble, whatever is right, whatever is pure, whatever is lovely, whatever is admirable—if anything is excellent or praiseworthy—think about such things. Whatever you have learned or received or heard from me, or seen in me—put it into practice. And the God of peace will be with you.

Philippians 4:4–9

What have you seen of Paul? What are you to copy? What is the promise of this type of walk?

> Do not fret—it only leads to evil.

Psalm 37:8

> Quiet down before God,
>   be prayerful before him.

Psalm 37:7 Message

**In my meantime place, I am learning . . .**

_____

_____

_____

_____

_____

**In my meantime place, God is requiring me to . . .**

_____

_____

_____

_____

_____

### Prayer

_Father, I am good at worrying, fretting, and all things related. I have practiced it way too long. I desire in this current situation not to worry and to trust you instead. Be my guide. Help me to filter my negative perceptions and bring them to the light of truth and trust. Calm my heart and quiet my mouth. In your name, amen._

# 23

## Look for the Good
## and Practice Dwelling There

*Learn the Pathway to Peace*

Finally, . . . whatever is true, whatever is noble, whatever is right, whatever is pure, whatever is lovely, whatever is admirable—if anything is excellent or praiseworthy—think about such things. . . . And the God of peace will be with you. . . . And my God will meet all your needs according to the riches of his glory in Christ Jesus.

Philippians 4:8–9, 19

From the very beginning God has had plans for us, wonderful plans to conform us into his image so we can give our best for his glory, or as Oswald Chambers says, our utmost for his highest.

Many times our dysfunctions, hurts, and ways of reacting to life keep us from allowing God access to the part of us that most needs to be changed. Often our meantime trials are small things that loom big to us because we have issues that God needs to heal and deliver us from. I have had many of these issues, but I want to share one with you that has been miraculously changed by my paying attention to what Scripture says in Philippians.

I used to have birthday issues. I don't know what else to call it. I just know that my birthdays were like a strange black cloud of sadness, disappointment, and unmet expectations—and this started while I was still young! I tried to figure it out, tried to make myself respond differently, but like clockwork, my emotional self would go into a terrible place several days before my birthday and would not leave until the day was over.

No one could make me happy, and no amount of attention would suffice. Without realizing I was the problem, I sabotaged every attempt and every well wisher. I tried to stuff it and hide it, but most people close to me knew I was disappointed each and every birthday. I tried counseling—and got even more stressed and confused by my dysfunction. And though it was undoubtedly something from my past, nothing seemed to ease the pain. I felt stuck. So for me, there was a meantime that I did not know how to live in, and it came each year.

When my disappointment began affecting my husband and children, I began to pray in earnest that God would heal whatever was within me that was so messed up in this area. Then as the date grew nearer, I had an idea. I would try to remember something good, try to focus on only the positive, try something different. And so I did. My mind quickly went to Philippians and what Paul instructed in chapter 4:

Whatever is true, whatever is noble, whatever is right, whatever is pure, whatever is lovely, whatever is admirable—if anything is excellent or praiseworthy—think about such things. Whatever you have learned or received or heard from me, or seen in me—put it into practice. And the God of peace will be with you.

verses 8–9

What has Paul been teaching the people? I keep repeating the main things because he too repeated them. I guess they must bear repeating.

- Whatever happens, watch your life and conduct (Phil. 1:27).
- Resist complaining and look past yourself (Phil. 2:14, 21).
- Practice perspective (Phil. 3:15–20).
- Rejoice and find joy in the Lord (Phil. 4:4).
- Acknowledge good and dwell there (Phil. 4:8).

For me, learning to live in the meantime of my birthday by focusing my mind on good was more than the answer. It freed me. I suppose I always wanted to do something special for my birthday, didn't know how to ask for it, and was chronically disappointed when the day did not match my expectations. So I decided to remember people I loved and planned my own party. The first year I invited ten friends. Instead of expecting them to celebrate me, I would spend my day celebrating them. I spent the month before my birthday planning and preparing. Rather than asking for gifts, I began picking out individual gifts for each one of them. I began losing myself and the pain in my focus on others. It was so much fun that I forgot to be upset, expectant, or sad.

On my birthday, I had a beautifully set table and a breakfast I had prepared. Each woman opened her gift individually. After each gift, I explained why I had chosen the gift and how much that person meant to me.

I continued that party for a few years, and guess what? It broke the power of the negative habit of dreading my birth date. No longer stuck, I have been reminded to use this meantime principle in other areas that I am having trouble getting through.

What are you dealing with in your life right now? How can you make a move to turn it around in the areas that depend on you?

We can start dealing with our negative thoughts by first controlling our mouth. Begin to cut out negative words and replace them with positive ones. This will be difficult at first if you're tempted to complain all the time. Just know that if you complain verbally, you will tend to be a negative thinker and person—and your meantime will become more miserable than it has to be.

Ask yourself some questions:

- Do I have peace, real peace, even though life is hard?
- Am I living as the best self that Christ's death has paid for me to be? Or am I giving in to every negative fear and doubt?
- If I am not living in a good place, what is holding me back?
- Do I have anyone to talk to, process and pray with, and hold me accountable?
- Have I asked God for a plan as I walk through this time?
- Do I have trouble seeing good? If so, why?
- Am I focused on progress or perfection?
- Do I have eyes to see that God is working change in me?

I am not Paul, but take it from me—we can sabotage the good God is trying to bestow. We can be our own worst enemy. We all ultimately choose how we will live. God, in his power, is our helper through the Holy Spirit, but we have to open the door, open the gift. That part is up to us—the healing is up to God. I heard it said once that we are to pray toward heaven and row toward the shore. Let's make sure we are praying and make sure we keep rowing.

Take your current situation and process it in light of the truth in God's Word:

For I have learned to be content whatever the circumstances.

Philippians 4:11

The Lord is my shepherd, I lack nothing.

Psalm 23:1

Goodness and love will follow me
all the days of my life.

Psalm 23:6

And now one last challenge for living in the meantime: receive peace. Let it settle you, even when there is not a solution today. Paul's closing thoughts:

I have learned to be content whatever the circumstances. I know what it is to be in need, and I know what it is to have plenty. I have learned the secret of being content in any and every situation, whether well fed or hungry, whether living in plenty or in want. I can do all this through him who gives me strength. . . . And my God will meet all your needs according to the riches of his glory in Christ Jesus.

Philippians 4:11–13, 19

He learned to live a "whatever" life. I want to learn to live that life too. Whatever happened, he lived for Christ and trusted Christ. When trouble was hard to bear, he kept reaffirming God's work and plan. When what he had was more than enough, he kept his focus and watched his perspective. And in the final outcome, he learned that refusing to worry and praying with trust brought peace greater than one can know on his or her own. With this peace, he lived in God confidence, knowing that he could do anything because he had the strength of Christ within him, knowing that because of God's love all his needs would be taken care of—from here to eternity and in every space in between.

Dwell on the person God wants you to become—escape from the limitations of the current moment and shine your spotlight on your full potential.

Tommy Newberry[1]

**In my meantime place, I am learning . . .**

_____

_____

_____

_____

_____

**In my meantime place, God is requiring me to . . .**

_____

_____

_____

_____

_____

### Prayer

_Lord, I want your peace. I also want others to experience your peace. Show me how I prevent your peace from penetrating my life when I refuse to look for good and refuse to follow the principles set before me in Scripture. Jesus, transform me into the image of Christ, that I might live as my best self in your power and for your glory. Amen._

# Conclusion

*Where Do We Go from Here?*

Life and how we process it have everything to do with the attitude we choose each day. We can walk through the difficult times grumpy and negative, or we can choose to hang on to the affirming promises of God's Word, even when life is hard.

This morning, as I finish this book, I am in pain. If you have been in pain, you know it's not fun. Yesterday I pulled a muscle in my back and can hardly breathe or move. However, as I woke up with my pain and began grumbling, I suddenly stopped the negative attitude by praising God, out loud. I began to thank him that he is with me in the pain, he is the healer of my body, and he will always be faithful to me, even in the challenges of life. In other words, I began thanking him because he is God and he is good!

I have no idea how long I will be down or how long it will take me to feel better. So in the meantime, I plan to continue praising him, thanking him that he is always at work in me, and holding on to his Word rather than leaning on my own understanding. In other words, my plan is to trust, then trust some more. This morning the praise was through tears of pain, but I was still praising and my attitude lifted to incredible joy.

It is my prayer that you will discover what God wants to change in you as a result of your current meantime path. I have included Scripture passages in appendix A to help you navigate, process, and find your way to freedom. They are promises from God's Word. They are for you, for me, and for all who choose to believe. They will be praise-starters as you learn to claim them and find peace because of them, no matter what your situation. Finally, this isn't a prayer but a gentle nudge. Life is hard, so choose wisely, pray frequently, and trust the bigger picture, planned by a big God!

Bless you!

Appendix A

# Scripture Passages for Trusting God in the Meantimes of Life

## Anger

Do not be quickly provoked in your spirit,
for anger resides in the lap of fools. (Eccles. 7:9)

My dear brothers and sisters, take note of this: Everyone should be quick to listen, slow to speak and slow to become angry, because human anger does not produce the righteousness that God desires. (James 1:19–20)

A quick-tempered person does foolish things.
(Prov. 14:17)

A hot-tempered person stirs up conflict,
but the one who is patient calms a quarrel.
(Prov. 15:18)

Refrain from anger and turn from wrath;
do not fret—it leads only to evil. (Ps. 37:8)

## Belief

For God so loved the world that he gave his one and only Son, that whoever believes in him shall not perish but have eternal life. (John 3:16)

Yet to all who did receive him, to those who believed in his name, he gave the right to become children of God. (John 1:12)

I have come into the world as a light, so that no one who believes in me should stay in darkness. (John 12:46)

Then Jesus declared, "I am the bread of life. Whoever comes to me will never go hungry, and whoever believes in me will never be thirsty." (John 6:35)

Everything is possible for one who believes. (Mark 9:23)

## Bitterness

I am disgusted with my life.
    Let me complain freely.
My bitter soul must complain. (Job 10:1 NLT)

People ruin their lives by their own foolishness
    and then are angry at the LORD. (Prov. 19:3 NLT)

Repent of your wickedness and pray to the Lord. Perhaps he will forgive your evil thoughts, for I can see that you are full of bitter jealousy and are held captive by sin. (Acts 8:22–23 NLT)

Surely resentment destroys the fool,
    and jealousy kills the simple. (Job 5:2 NLT)

Get rid of all bitterness, rage, anger, harsh words, and slander, as well as all types of evil behavior. Instead, be kind to each

other, tenderhearted, forgiving one another, just as God through
Christ has forgiven you. (Eph. 4:31–32 NLT)

## Children

They replied, "Believe in the Lord Jesus, and you will be saved—
you and your household." (Acts 16:31)

> For I will pour water on the thirsty land,
>   and streams on the dry ground;
> I will pour out my Spirit on your offspring,
>   and my blessing on your descendants. (Isa. 44:3)

> Discipline your son, and he will give you peace;
> he will bring delight to your soul. (Prov. 29:17)

## Comfort

> Though I walk in the midst of trouble,
>   you preserve my life.
> You stretch out your hand against the anger of my foes,
>   with your right hand you save me. (Ps. 138:7)

> Though he may stumble, he will not fall,
> for the LORD upholds him with his hand. (Ps. 37:24)

> The LORD is good,
>   a refuge in times of trouble.
> He cares for those who trust in him. (Nah. 1:7)

> Cast your cares on the LORD
>   and he will sustain you;
> he will never let
>   the righteous be shaken. (Ps. 55:22)

Come to me, all you who are weary and burdened, and I will give you rest. (Matt. 11:28)

> Wait for the LORD;
> be strong and take heart
> and wait for the LORD. (Ps. 27:14)

## Contentment

> A cheerful heart is good medicine,
> but a crushed spirit dries up the bones. (Prov. 17:22)

Keep your lives free from the love of money and be content with what you have, because God has said, "Never will I leave you; never will I forsake you." (Heb. 13:5)

> A heart at peace gives life to the body,
> but envy rots the bones. (Prov. 14:30)

Godliness with contentment is great gain. (1 Tim. 6:6)

## Death

> Even though I walk
>     through the darkest valley,
> I will fear no evil,
>     for you are with me;
> your rod and your staff,
>     they comfort me. (Ps. 23:4)

> When calamity comes, the wicked are brought down,
> but even in death the righteous seek refuge in God.
>         (Prov. 14:32)

For this God is our God for ever and ever;
he will be our guide even to the end. (Ps. 48:14)

But God will redeem me from the realm of the dead;
he will surely take me to himself. (Ps. 49:15)

He will swallow up death forever.
The Sovereign LORD will wipe away the tears
from all faces. (Isa. 25:8)

Though outwardly we are wasting away, yet inwardly we are
being renewed day by day. (2 Cor. 4:16)

For I am convinced that neither death nor life, neither angels
nor demons, neither the present nor the future, nor any powers,
neither height nor depth, nor anything else in all creation, will
be able to separate us from the love of God that is in Christ Jesus
our Lord. (Rom. 8:38–39)

## Enemies

The LORD will grant that the enemies who rise up against you
will be defeated before you. They will come at you from one
direction but flee from you in seven. (Deut. 28:7)

For the LORD your God is the one who goes with you to fight
for you against your enemies to give you victory. (Deut. 20:4)

"No weapon forged against you will prevail,
and you will refute every tongue that accuses you.
This is the heritage of the servants of the LORD,
and this is their vindication from me," declares the
LORD. (Isa. 54:17)

The LORD is with me; he is my helper.
I will look in triumph on my enemies. (Ps. 118:7)

> Their hearts are secure, they will have no fear;
>> in the end they will look in triumph on their foes.
>>> (Ps. 112:8)

## Faith

If any of you lacks wisdom, you should ask God, who gives generously to all without finding fault, and it will be given to you. But when you ask, you must believe and not doubt, because the one who doubts is like a wave of the sea, blown and tossed by the wind. (James 1:5–6)

So then, just as you received Christ Jesus as Lord, continue to live your lives in him, rooted and built up in him, strengthened in the faith as you were taught, and overflowing with thankfulness. (Col. 2:6–7)

Be on your guard; stand firm in the faith; be courageous; be strong. (1 Cor. 16:13)

I tell you the truth, anyone who has faith in me will do what I have been doing. He will do even greater things than these, because I am going to the Father. And I will do whatever you ask in my name, so that the Son may bring glory to the Father. (John 14:12–13)

For in the gospel a righteousness from God is revealed, a righteousness that is by faith from first to last, just as it is written: "The righteous will live by faith." (Rom. 1:17)

So do not throw away your confidence; it will be richly rewarded. You need to persevere so that when you have done the will of God, you will receive what he has promised. (Heb. 10:35–36)

My righteous one will live by faith. And if he shrinks back, I will not be pleased with him. (Heb. 10:38)

And without faith it is impossible to please God, because anyone who comes to him must believe that he exists and that he rewards those who earnestly seek him. (Heb. 11:6)

## Fear

> For I am the LORD your God,
> who takes hold of your right hand
> and says to you, Do not fear;
> I will help you. (Isa. 41:13)

For the Spirit God gave us does not make us timid, but gives us power, love and self-discipline. (2 Tim. 1:7)

> God is our refuge and strength,
> an ever-present help in trouble. (Ps. 46:1)

> Fear of man will prove to be a snare,
> but whoever trusts in the LORD is kept safe. (Prov. 29:25)

> The LORD is my light and my salvation—
> whom shall I fear?
> The LORD is the stronghold of my life—
> of whom shall I be afraid? . . .
> Though an army besiege me,
> my heart will not fear;
> though war break out against me,
> even then will I be confident. (Ps. 27:1, 3)

> He will have no fear of bad news;
> his heart is steadfast, trusting in the LORD. (Ps. 112:7)

> So do not fear, for I am with you;
> do not be dismayed, for I am your God.
> I will strengthen you and help you;
> I will uphold you with my righteous right hand.
> (Isa. 41:10)

But now, this is what the LORD says—
   he who created you, O Jacob,
   he who formed you, O Israel:
"Fear not, for I have redeemed you;
   I have summoned you by name; you are mine.
When you pass through the waters,
   I will be with you;
and when you pass through the rivers,
   they will not sweep over you.
When you walk through the fire,
   you will not be burned;
   the flames will not set you ablaze.
For I am the LORD, your God,
   the Holy One of Israel, your Savior. (Isa. 43:1–3)

And even the very hairs of your head are all numbered. So don't be afraid; you are worth more than many sparrows. (Matt. 10:30–31)

Peace I leave with you; my peace I give you. I do not give to you as the world gives. Do not let your hearts be troubled and do not be afraid. (John 14:27)

## Guidance

Whether you turn to the right or to the left, your ears will hear a voice behind you, saying, "This is the way; walk in it." (Isa. 30:21)

For this God is our God for ever and ever;
   he will be our guide even to the end. (Ps. 48:14)

In their hearts humans plan their course,
   but the LORD establishes their steps. (Prov. 16:9)

In all your ways submit to him,
   and he will make your paths straight. (Prov. 3:6)

I will instruct you and teach you in the way you should
  go;
  I will counsel you with my loving eye on you. (Ps. 32:8)

## Help in Troubles

The LORD is good,
  a refuge in times of trouble.
  He cares for those who trust in him. (Nah. 1:7)

You are my hiding place;
  you will protect me from trouble
  and surround me with songs of deliverance. (Ps. 32:7)

Why, my soul, are you downcast?
  Why so disturbed within me?
Put your hope in God,
  for I will yet praise him,
  my Savior and my God. (Ps. 42:11)

My flesh and my heart may fail,
but God is the strength of my heart
and my portion forever. (Ps. 73:26)

No harm will overtake you,
no disaster will come near your tent.
For he will command his angels concerning you
to guard you in all your ways. (Ps. 91:10–11)

The LORD is a refuge for the oppressed,
  a stronghold in times of trouble. (Ps. 9:9)

You, LORD, keep my lamp burning;
my God turns my darkness into light. (Ps. 18:28)

## Life Losses

> You have turned my mourning into joyful dancing.
> > You have taken away my clothes of mourning and
> > > clothed me with joy,
> that I might sing praises to you and not be silent.
> > O Lord my God, I will give you thanks forever!
> > > (Ps. 30:11–12 NLT)

> He heals the brokenhearted
> > and bandages their wounds. (Ps. 147:3 NLT)

> God blesses those who mourn,
> > for they will be comforted. (Matt. 5:4 NLT)

All praise to God, the Father of our Lord Jesus Christ. God is our merciful Father and the source of all comfort. (2 Cor. 1:3 NLT)

## Needs

> As soon as I pray, you answer me;
> > you encourage me by giving me strength. (Ps. 138:3
> > > NLT)

Let us come boldly to the throne of our gracious God. There we will receive his mercy, and we will find grace to help us when we need it most. (Heb. 4:16 NLT)

If you need wisdom, ask our generous God, and he will give it to you. (James 1:5 NLT)

Seek the kingdom of God above all else, and live righteously, and he will give you everything you need. (Matt. 6:33 NLT)

God will generously provide all you need. Then you will always have everything you need and plenty left over to share with others. (2 Cor. 9:8 NLT)

## Peace

> I will lie down and sleep in peace,
>     for you alone, O LORD,
>         make me dwell in safety. (Ps. 4:8)

> The LORD gives strength to his people;
>     the LORD blesses his people with peace. (Ps. 29:11)

> Great peace have they who love your law,
>     and nothing can make them stumble. (Ps. 119:165)

> When a man's ways are pleasing to the LORD,
>     he makes even his enemies live at peace with him.
>         (Prov. 16:7)

> You will keep in perfect peace
> him whose mind is steadfast,
> because he trusts in you. (Isa. 26:3)

The mind of the sinful man is death, but the mind controlled by the Spirit is life and peace. (Rom. 8:6)

Peace I leave with you; my peace I give you. I do not give as the world gives. Do not let your hearts be troubled and do not be afraid. (John 14:27)

For he himself is our peace. (Eph. 2:14)

## Trust

God is our refuge and strength,
an ever-present help in trouble.
Therefore we will not fear, though the earth give way
and the mountains fall into the heart of the sea.
(Ps. 46:1–2)

For the Lord God is a sun and shield;
the Lord bestows favor and honor;
no good thing does he withhold
from those whose walk is blameless.
Lord Almighty,
blessed is the one who trusts in you. (Ps. 84:11–12)

Trust in the Lord and do good;
dwell in the land and enjoy safe pasture.
Take delight in the Lord,
and he will give you the desires of your heart.
Commit your way to the Lord;
trust in him and he will do this. (Ps. 37:3–5)

Trust in the Lord with all your heart
and lean not on your own understanding;
in all your ways submit to him,
and he will make your paths straight. (Prov. 3:5–6)

# Appendix B

# Sitting with the Truths of Philippians

*Five-Week Bible Study Resource*

This study guide will help you "sit in Philippians" so that you can process why Paul wrote this letter to his friends in Philippi and connect with how it can be meaningful to you today. It is meant to be a complement to what you read in this book's chapters, as Philippians can help change your perspective on living in the meantime—especially if and when life is not pleasant.

You can do this study after reading the book or while you are reading it. You can process the material by yourself or with a group of women. The guide can be adapted for a home group or class, with five weeks of study and either an opening week or a closing week over a shared meal.

Keep in mind that the goal is not for you just to fill in the blanks; rather, the goal is to encourage you to connect with God through the truth of his Word. You are encouraged to read, process, pray, and learn to walk out the truths in your daily life.

## Studying a Book of the Bible

When preparing to study a book of the Bible, the first step is reading the book through in its entirety. Do this to gain an understanding of the context in which it was written. It is often helpful to do this a few times and to read the book in your regular version of choice, such as the NIV, and then in another version, such as the Message or the New Living Translation.

A simple approach to studying God's Word involves three steps:[1]

Step 1: *Observation*: What does the passage say?

Step 2: *Interpretation*: What does the passage mean?

Step 3: *Application*: What am I going to do about what the passage says and means?

Observation: Look for important terms and repeated phrases. Look for relationships between ideas—cause and effect, ifs and thens, questions and answers, comparisons and contrasts.

Interpretation: Let Scripture interpret Scripture. Let other passages shed light on the passage you are looking at. Use the cross-references noted in your Bible. The Bible was written long ago, and when we interpret it, we must try to understand the writer's cultural context.

Application: This is why we study the Bible. We want our lives to change, and we want to be obedient to God. The application step is putting into practice what God has taught you in your study. This is the most important part of Bible study.

## Paul's Letter

The book of Philippians is a letter written by Paul to the church in Philippi. It is Paul's joy letter, written from, of all places, his jail cell. In this letter, we can see an exploration of what it means to experience contentment and joy even in life's most difficult circumstances. Paul's primary goal in this letter was to challenge the Christians to rejoice regardless of the circumstances around them. He knew they could do this only if they believed and lived in the reality of God being at work in every circumstance of life. We may find it difficult to rejoice *for* every situation, but we can rejoice *in* everything because we know that nothing is outside of God's control. In each chapter of Philippians, Paul returns again and again to the theme of Christian joy.

## Outline of Paul's Letter to the Philippians[2]

### Chapter 1: The Christian Purpose—to live is Christ (1:21)

Paul's life was not perfect. He faced many harsh and difficult circumstances. But even in the worst of times, God was near to Paul's heart and thoughts and was the very presence that defined his life. He was living life in Christ. We too can learn how to live our life in Christ, with Christ as our life.

### Chapter 2: The Christian Pattern—the mind of Christ (2:5–8)

Paul put an emphasis on unity, humility, and a new attitude for living. Being part of a Christian community was something Paul did not take lightly. He encouraged the Christians to love sincerely and to live humbly before others and God. He knew that this new pattern of attitude and life would take practice, obedience, and the strength and grace of God working in people's lives. We can all relate to needing the presence and power of God to live differently, with a new mind in this life.

### Chapter 3: The Christian's Prize—the prize of the high calling (3:14)

Paul begins this chapter with a simple instruction: rejoice! But this instruction is not simple in the real world, where people live imperfect lives, connected to imperfect people, death, disease, and difficulties. Yet, Paul urges believers to take hold of what is important and press toward the prize of their high calling. This is a reminder we all need in our everyday lives.

### Chapter 4: The Christian's Provision—all things through Christ; Christ will supply every need (4:13, 19)

Paul ends his letter to the church in Philippi by challenging the Christians to stand firm regardless of their circumstances. He reminds them of the truth that God will supply every provision, and he exhorts them to keep their minds on what is good. Paul looked for the good within every circumstance in which he found himself. If there was nothing good that he could see, he stood on the belief that God himself was good enough. This ending exhortation of prayer, praise, and thanksgiving is a key to living the life God designed for us.

## The Practice of Processing Scripture

As you do each lesson, you will read a passage and then jot down some thoughts or, as some call it, journal. You will be asked to think about what Paul's letter is saying, how it can be translated to your life today, and how it can make a difference in your understanding of living out the Christian life. The focus will be on how you can learn to trust God in every meantime circumstance and frustration. Biblical truth leads the way as it gives an anchor and promise for our hope—it gives us something to focus on as we are learning to believe, really believe, that God is always at work in us. Then you will pray the passage back to God, using its truth as your guide.

### Read the Passage

If possible, read the passage out loud. As you read, underline or highlight any verse in the passage that is meaningful to you.

### Journal about the Passage

Write out your thoughts about the verses you highlighted.

### Pray the Passage

Pray the verses back to God as an exercise of praying God's Word. Use the truth in the verses as your guide.

### Example

Read: "being confident of this, that he who began a good work in you will carry it on to completion until the day of Christ Jesus" (Phil. 1:6).

Journal: Sometimes it seems like my life has a million loose ends. I don't see any progress and can easily feel like a failure as I slip back into old routines, habits, or reactions to life. This verse is a comfort because it promises something God will do in me. According to this verse, God will complete me! He started a good work, and now he will finish it.

Pray: Father, I thank you that I can place all my confidence in you. You alone are the power at work in me to finish the good work you started the day I gave my life to you. Thank you, Lord, that you are always working in me and that it is your job to complete your work in me. Thank you that your work is being done even now. Thank you that I can rest in your work within me and trust in you not to leave a single thing left untouched by your Spirit's power. I am a work in process, and you are a God who is always working to complete me.

Let's begin!

# Lesson 1
## God Completes His Work in You

### Overview of Philippians

Shut out every other thought and keep yourself before God in this one thing only—my utmost for His highest. I am determined to be absolutely and entirely for Him and Him alone.

Oswald Chambers[3]

### Read A Woman Who Trusts God, Chapters 1–5

### Read the Book of Philippians

Read the entire book of Philippians straight through. Do not stop to underline or highlight (there will be time for that later). Read for understanding and flow of the entire letter. If someone wrote you a letter, you would read it start to finish before going through it line by line and picking it apart. The same is true here. This is a letter and must be read in its entirety to start our study.

Keep in mind that Paul was writing to people like us who had real struggles. They gravitated to fear and worry too. Like a wise and trusted friend, Paul writes them a letter to encourage them to have peace as they trust God with all outcomes. He normalizes trials and challenges by reminding them of his struggles, and he exhorts them to live in a place of joy—a place that can be lived in only as we keep our minds on God and stay focused on his active work within us.

As I sat with the entire letter for a while, truths began to pop out at me. Ask God for the same in your reading.

### Servants of Christ Jesus: Philippians 1:1–9

The letter starts by saying it is from Paul and Timothy. References to Paul's journeys in the book of Acts help us conclude that Paul was the primary writer. The letter opens with no reference to Paul's position. This is unlike his other letters, which open with reference to his apostleship.[4] This letter obviously begins more like a warm embrace written by a servant or slave of Christ Jesus. It mixes humble submission with highest honor.

Paul and Timothy are identified by the word *servant* in verse 1. Look up *servant* in the dictionary and write out what it means:

_____

_____

It is interesting to note that Paul defines himself as a person living his life for another—that other being Christ his Lord and by extension the body of Christ. This is Paul's new identity. He tells believers of his previous identity in Philippians 3:4–7. Before Christ, Paul was recognized for his good works and pedigree. Now, by knowing Christ intimately, he thinks everything besides Christ alone is worthless, simply stating that he is a servant of Christ or a slave of a master. Basically, in today's terms, he is saying, "I belong to Christ. I am his."

We live in a culture that teaches us from a young age the importance of finding ourselves and living our lives true to ourselves. The first thing we learn is how to put self first. We grow up with unrealistic expectations that are focused on meeting our own needs, and we commit to Christ based on comfort, while praying for blessing and things to make our lives easier. This does not sound like a slave to me. This sounds like a spoiled child who wants things her way.

How can we turn our lives around so that our definition would be different?

In viewing your identity and your life circumstances, is your mind focused on God or on self?

Here is how I define myself when I am focused on self: Debbie, a woman who is living to make the best of herself so that others will commit to making her happy and life will meet her every expectation. Debbie, a Christian woman who will serve God if she agrees with, is comfortable with, or feels confident in the job he calls her to. Debbie, who will love others in God's strength when she deems them important, feels warm and fuzzy around them, or needs them for something.

Here is how I define myself according to God's design for me: Debbie, a woman belonging to God, committed to serving him even when she doesn't understand. Debbie, a woman committed to humbling her heart, life, attitudes, and relationships before God for his purposes, living as one enslaved to the God who set her free and redeemed her. Debbie, a woman who commits her past, present, and future to the God who created her and who cares for her, living life with Christ as her Lord, even in the darkest place, the darkest days, and the most inconvenient and troubling of times.

Now write your definition:

_____

_____

_____

_____

## The Christians in Philippi as Saints

Paul calls the Christians in Philippi saints. Saints are those who have been set apart or sanctified. They are different. The difference is seen not in pointless eccentricity but in the fact that they are consecrated to Christ and his service. They are devoted to God. "Saints are not dead people who have been deceased long enough for defects to be forgotten. They are people who are very much alive both physically and spiritually. They may be clumsy novices in the faith. They may yet wear the 'swaddling clothes' of initial obedience to the gospel. But they are saints. That simply means they have been set apart from sin and for service."[5]

What does being set apart mean to you? Are there areas in your life that need to be set apart and surrendered to Christ for his use?

## Grace and Peace

The letter opens with the words *grace* and *peace*. According to *Webster's Dictionary*, grace is "divine love and protection given to man by God; good will and favor." Peace is "a state of harmony, freedom, and security." In the Greek, grace (*charis*) is favor, benefit, blessing, good will, offering, privilege. Peace (*eirene*) is safety, blessing, to wish one well.

Paul's greeting combines Greek and Jewish thought. *Charis* is related to the English word "charm." The basic idea in *charis* is brightness and beauty. While retaining this, *charis* in New Testament usage means God's eager love reaching out through Christ to give deliverance that cannot be earned or merited. It is

God's unmerited favor toward us. The word *peace* is the Jewish word for total well-being.

Grace and peace—God's love, beauty, and brightness along with total well-being.

When you are in turmoil, trouble, or the meantime, how does it threaten your peace? In these hard spots, does the grace of God appear real to you? Why or why not?

## Paul's Confidence

Are you in a tough spot right now? Do you have a tendency to go from A to Z in record speed? Perhaps you need some interval training. As you study Philippians, keep your own meantime in mind as you read. Try to think of yourself as learning how to live biblically in the interval between the onset of trouble and the solution to your problem.

Paul was confident in Christ, and we see this confidence throughout the New Testament letters written by Paul to the church. One to take note of is in 2 Corinthians 4:7–5:9.

Turn to that passage and read it slowly, taking in what Paul was communicating about confidence in God.

What does Paul compare us to in verse 7?

According to Paul's account of hardships, do you think they are a normal part of our life here on earth or just for a select few?

_____

_____

_____

_____

Verse 16 begins with a "therefore"; what is that "therefore" referring to? And, what is Paul's instructional encouragement in the rest of the passage?

_____

_____

_____

_____

In what confidence are we to live? And, in what way are we to walk out our lives? (5:7)

_____

_____

_____

_____

### A Theme to Remember: Problems Are Inevitable but Living Overwhelmed Is Optional

Romans 8:35–37 is a good passage to memorize. The meantime often tempts us to feel like God has forgotten us. But we are not alone. Nothing can separate us from the God who loves us.

Throughout our lives we will go through stuff. Some of it will be large and other things small, maybe even petty. Regardless of size or intensity of problems, they are still something we must learn how to maneuver as a believer in Jesus Christ. In

Matthew 6, Jesus talks about how pagans (unbelieving people) have little faith, and because of that they spin their wheels worrying about all the outward trappings and provisions of this life. He makes it very clear that we do not have to be that kind of people, instead we can live by faith and with our trust in a God who knows exactly what we need.

As you close this lesson, read that account of the words of Christ, Matthew 6:19–34.

What stands out the most for you personally?

_____

_____

_____

_____

What is it that God is speaking to you through the words of Christ?

_____

_____

_____

_____

How can this move you to more of the confidence and trust that Paul lived in and experienced?

_____

_____

_____

_____

# Lesson 2
## God Is Working through the Hard Stuff

*Philippians 1:12–30*

He asks us to be our utmost for Him and we begin to debate.
He then providentially produces a crisis where we have to de-
cide—for or against. That moment becomes a great crossroads
in our lives.

Oswald Chambers[6]

### Read *A Woman Who Trusts God*, Chapters 6–10

### Read Philippians 1:12–30

Highlight any verse that speaks to you about trusting God with
all outcomes. Look for key words, phrases, and themes. Now
write out your thoughts about the verses you highlighted.

_____

_____

_____

_____

_____

Pray the verses back to God using your thoughts.

A theme that means so much to me personally is that things
happen *to* me so something can happen *in* me. What is happening in your life right now? Could it be that even though it
is difficult God will use it to produce something good in you?
Paul was in chains, but he trusted that the very thing happening
to him would turn out to deliver him into something better.

**Paul's Situation**

Let's recall Paul's situation (Phil. 1:1–19) as we answer some questions.

Look up the word *rejoice*. What should have stopped Paul from rejoicing? What happened to him? Think in detail.

_____

_____

_____

_____

What condition was Paul in when he wrote these words? Use adjectives. Think about how it must have been for him.

_____

_____

_____

_____

Philippians is considered Paul's joy letter, yet he speaks from chains. How is he able to have joy in adversity? Read James 1:2–4. What does James say about your troubles?

- Trials _____ my faith.
- Testing _____ perseverance.
- Perseverance works in me so that I become _____, _____, and not _____ anything.

What circumstantial chains have you been in lately? How have your current struggles locked you up?

_____

_____

_____

_____

What effects do these hard times have on you?

_____

_____

_____

_____

How can your problems serve a purpose of spiritual advancement?

_____

_____

_____

_____

What attitude does it appear that Paul had in his troubles?

_____

_____

_____

_____

Did Paul's situation and attitude affect the entire palace? Does your attitude affect your home, your workplace, your palace?

Read Philippians 1:20. What would sufficient courage look like in your situation?

Read Philippians 1:21. Is there a circumstance in your life that you might need to let the reins loose on?

Read Philippians 1:27. Paul tells the Philippians to conduct themselves in a manner worthy of the gospel. What does this mean to you?

### Suffering for Christ

Read Philippians 1:29–30. To believe means to accept as real or true, to hold fast. To suffer means to endure or feel distress or pain; to sustain damage, injury, or loss; to undergo experiences.

Finish the following sentences. To believe on Christ means I . . .

_____

_____

_____

_____

To suffer for Christ means I . . .

_____

_____

_____

_____

God has granted that you will suffer. What does that mean to you?

_____

_____

_____

_____

What do you suppose the outcome of a personal struggle would be according to Paul?

_____

_____

_____

_____

Read Acts 14:21–22. Why did the disciples need to be encouraged?

_____

_____

_____

_____

Were they told there would be just a few bumps in the road?

_____

_____

_____

_____

Read about one of Paul's missionary trips in 1 Thessalonians 2:2–8. How did Paul manage to continue on despite strong opposition?

_____

_____

_____

_____

Do you ever experience strong opposition?

_____

_____

_____

_____

Difficult circumstances and suffering can change us. Paul tells the Philippians that the Christian life is a journey of trust and belief but also of suffering. It would be great to live on some

221

glory mountain, but that is not real life. Real life has real suffering, and Paul was clear in teaching the people the truth and how to walk it out on the real streets of life.

### God Finishes His Work—I Am His Work

Read Psalm 138:8. What are the key words/phrases in this verse? What do the key words say to you as encouragement? Write this verse out on a 3x5 index card and make a point to thank God for the truth several times a week.

---
---
---

Read Psalm 51:10–12. Write it into a prayer, knowing that we need a pure heart in order to share in Christian love, fellowship, and faith with those God puts in our lives. When we are in the middle of a crisis, it is often difficult to focus on how we treat others, but it will help us keep our priorities straight.

---
---
---

Now read Isaiah 9:6 and turn that into a prayer of praise for who God is in your life.

---
---
---

List the four things in Isaiah 9:6 that Christ came to be in your life. What do each of them mean to you today?

_____

_____

_____

_____

_____

## A Theme to Remember: You Are Not Alone

Do you ever feel like God has forgotten you? You are walking along humming your favorite song, and then all of a sudden, out of nowhere life happens and leaves you hanging in midair. You are somewhere between the reality of the real world and the promises God has made to you. The space in between your circumstances and the promise of God's faithfulness is the meantime. Throughout Philippians, Paul teaches us how to live in that space we call the meantime. As we study together, we will keep going back to the question, How do I live in the meantime?

# Lesson 3
## Living for Christ

*Philippians 2:1–3:14*

It's as if Paul were saying, "My determined purpose is to be my utmost for His highest—my best for His glory."

Oswald Chambers[7]

### Read *A Woman Who Trusts God*, Chapters 11–15

### Read Philippians 2:1–3:14

Highlight any verse that is meaningful to you. Now write out your thoughts about the verses you highlighted.

---

---

---

---

---

Pray the verses back to God using your thoughts.

### Being Like-Minded

Read Philippians 2:1–2. What did Paul say would make his joy complete in ministry to the Philippians?

---

---

---

---

What are the four things that he hoped they would have toward each other?

_____

_____

_____

_____

Look up definitions of each of the four things and jot them down next to each one.

### Putting Others First
Read Philippians 2:3–4. What instructions are given here?

_____

_____

_____

_____

### Every Knee Shall Bow
Read Philippians 2:5–14. How does this passage instruct us to live?

_____

_____

_____

### Instructions for Living
Read Philippians 2:12–21. What is God saying to you through each of the themes below:

work out your salvation with fear and trembling

_____

_____

God works in us to will and to act

_____

_____

do everything without grumbling

_____

_____

become blameless and pure

_____

_____

shine like stars

_____

_____

poured out like a drink offering

_____

_____

sacrifice and service coming from your faith

_____

_____

be glad and rejoice with me

_____

_____

everyone looks after their own interests

_____

_____

## Rejoice in the Lord!

Read Philippians 2:18 and 3:1. Look up the word *rejoice*. How does the meaning apply to you?

_____

_____

_____

_____

Look up the words *trouble* and *safeguard*. How does the word become practical in meaning and application?

_____

_____

_____

_____

One of the major steps in finding peace is learning what it means to rejoice. How do you train yourself to be glad or find joy in the Lord?

_____

_____

_____

_____

### Put No Confidence in the Flesh

Read Philippians 3:2–6. What is the theme? What is the passage saying?

_____

_____

_____

_____

What is Paul warning the people to watch out for? What did he call them? Why?

_____

_____

_____

_____

Paul was religious before he was saved, but his religion could not save him. Were you religious before being born again?

_____

_____

_____

_____

What is the difference in your relationship with God now?

_____

_____

_____

_____

Read Philippians 3:7–9. Write in your own words what Paul was saying.

_____

_____

_____

_____

Read Philippians 3:10–11 in a few different versions. What are you presently holding on to that might keep you from knowing Christ completely?

_____

_____

_____

_____

Read Philippians 3:12–14. What does pressing on mean to you? How do you lay a real-life problem down in order to go forward?

_____

_____

_____

_____

Do you ever struggle with the pride of believing that you have some things down pretty good, and because of that you are not as in tune to Scripture's truth? Here Paul says that he does not consider himself to have taken hold of all of the truth, but he keeps pressing on towards it.

Stop right now and ask God to make your relationship with him and the truth in his word fresh and new to you. Ask him to forgive you for taking any of it for granted and ask him to grant you a fresh start today.

## Life Lessons

Sum up this week's lesson with a list of life lessons that can be applied in your life.

Example: Difficult circumstances should not prevent us from sharing the gospel.

<br>

## A Theme to Remember: Practice Obedience One Step at a Time, Stepping out of Your Past and into His Future for You

Our walk with Christ is a daily one. We go through ups and downs, twists and turns, starts and stops. Some days it is a joy and a true experience of his Spirit within us, and other days we feel like perhaps we have made it all up in our silly little heads. Living for Christ is so much about our focus and very little about our feelings. And, though he came that we would know him in experience, we are not to base our days on experience but rather on faith in what Scripture tells us to be true. That is why it is important to lay down each day, at the end of each day, taking on a new morning as a breath of new beginning. If we make this a practice, we will begin to walk in relationship with God being mindful of his presence with us. We will be looking up instead of around and down. We will press on just as Paul is telling the people in Philippi to press on. It all happens one choice at a time, one step at a time, one day at a time.

# Lesson 4
## Press On with a New Perspective

*Philippians 3:15–4:9*

We are not meant to be seen as God's perfect, bright-shining examples, but to be seen as the everyday essence of ordinary life exhibiting the miracle of His grace.

Oswald Chambers[8]

### Read *A Woman Who Trusts God*, Chapters 16–19

### Read Philippians 3:15–4:9
Highlight any verse that is meaningful to you. Now write out your thoughts about the verses you highlighted.

_____

_____

_____

_____

_____

Pray the verses back to God using your thoughts.

### Spiritual Maturity
Philippians 3:15 speaks of spiritual maturity and the perspective or view we have when mature. How do we mature?

_____

_____

_____

_____

Philippians 3:16 tells us to walk in those things we have already learned. What are some things you have "learned" that you have trouble practicing when you go through a trial?

_____

_____

_____

_____

In Philippians 3:17–20, Paul speaks of patterns of living. So far Paul has been speaking of his pattern of trust. Describe this in your own words.

_____

_____

_____

_____

In this passage, he speaks of a different pattern, an ungodly pattern. What do those who live in that pattern have their minds set on?

_____

_____

_____

_____

Philippians 3:21 says God will transform our bodies. But until we are in our heavenly transformed bodies, we live here and now. Read Romans 12:1–2. How does God transform us while we live in the here and now?

_____

_____

_____

_____

**Standing Firm**

Based on Philippians 3:15–4:9, write out a pattern for standing firm in the Lord.

_____

_____

_____

_____

Here are three that are simple for me to remember:

1. Rejoice—look up and find joy in the truth that God is with me.
2. Press on—keep moving forward with doing the will of God in my daily life as my goal.
3. Perspective—watch my perspective and view. How am I framing my situation? Am I fretting or trusting? Do I believe that God has my life "framed" in grace and power, or am I believing that everything is awful and too difficult to bear?

Philippians 4:4–8 provides golden instructions. This is the pattern for us to learn to live in. Write about it in your own words and develop your own personal practices or steps to live this way—and press on to learn a new pattern of living!

_____

_____

_____

_____

_____

## A Theme to Remember: Watch Your Perspective, Learn to Reframe Your Circumstances with Truth

It is much easier for us to think the old ways we have always thought. Some call this our internal script, others call this our learned narrative, and others refer to this as our old tapes. Whatever you call it, be sure of this—all your life you have been developing patterns of thinking, reasoning, and reacting to life and problems. Some of this has been modeled by parents or influences that are not entirely healthy themselves. We learn to believe untruth and lies and things that are opposite of God's way of living, reasoning, and reacting. When we live out of our old framing, we often are skewed and of little faith. But, when we learn to take each "picture" that life brings us, framing it in the truth of God's faithfulness through all of life, we can then begin moving towards real spiritual maturity. This is not over-spiritualizing life, but it is putting our life, as lives in his care and keeping, into the proper perspective, or the proper frame.

# Lesson 5
# God Confidence—He Supplies All We Need

*Philippians 4:10–23*

Faith is not some weak and pitiful emotion, but is strong and vigorous confidence built on the fact that God is holy love.

Oswald Chambers[9]

## Read *A Woman Who Trusts God*, Chapters 20–23

## Read Philippians 4:10–23

Highlight any verse that is meaningful to you. Now write out your thoughts about the verses you highlighted.

_____

_____

_____

_____

_____

Pray the verses back to God using your thoughts.

## Pressing toward the Goal

As we begin this last lesson on Philippians, let's go back to the lifestyle of pressing on toward God and the goal of becoming more formed into the image of Jesus Christ.

In Philippians 3:12, identify the key words and look them up in a dictionary or concordance. Here are some suggestions:

obtained

perfect

press

take hold

Isn't it interesting that Paul states that he is not perfect? This was a man who had so much going for him. His pedigree was top-notch, and he certainly served in admirable ways, suffered as one filled with faith, and loved as one filled with grace. Yet, even Paul states that he has not yet been made perfect.

How do you feel about perfection? Do you ever struggle with an all-or-nothing mentality? If you do, how does this cross over into your relationship with God?

_____

_____

_____

_____

What was Paul pressing toward? What did his goal seem to be?

_____

_____

_____

_____

## Paul's Example

The goal of knowing Christ seemed to absorb all of Paul's energy. This is an example for us. Far too often we let anything and sometimes everything take our eyes off this goal. We can liken our walk with Christ to an athlete in training. We are in need of being single-minded.

What attitude, based on what you have read in his letter, contributed to Paul's lifestyle of contentment? What do you think the "secret" is?

_____

_____

_____

_____

Read Philippians 4:13. Often we view God's strength only as the strength God can give us. In light of all of chapter 4, how do you think Paul had the strength to do all things, live in any circumstance, or rejoice in difficult situations?

_____

_____

_____

_____

Read Philippians 4:19. What does this verse promise? Where does our provision come from? How can this keep us from worry?

_____

_____

_____

_____

Now summarize Paul's message in Philippians and how his pattern for living well in the meantime can be a pattern for you too.

_____

_____

_____

_____

### A Theme to Remember: Look for Good and Practice Dwelling There; Learn the Pathway to Peace

The entire letter to the church in Philippi points to one thing—trusting God with our lives. We are told that we are his saints, in his hands, created to be light, and given the ability to endure suffering as a means for Christ to be magnified within us. In this letter we are also given a pathway to living out our daily life. And, that pathway could possibly be summed up with a simple thing to remember—look for good and dwell there. Though the words are simple, the practice is not as easy to walk in real lives that are complicated with responsibilities, bills, troubles, relationships, hurts, illness, and the like. Still, in real life we can and must learn to rejoice in the God of our salvation by looking for good—looking for God, in all things.

As you close this study, stop and reflect on the Scripture you read, the themes you saw, and the instruction you have been given. Remember that Paul was real human flesh just like us. He made mistakes, had a sin nature, had to learn these same things that he taught others. Also remember that he did not write this letter from a spa but from prison. If someone in hard conditions could tell us that they were pressing on to maturity, how much more should we make it our goal to press on to all that Jesus Christ has for us. Let his light shine through you, as you are held out as hope in a very dark world that desperately needs the light.

# Notes

### Introduction

1. Oswald Chambers, *My Utmost for His Highest* (Grand Rapids: Discovery House Publishers, 1992), February 11.

### Chapter 2: Problems Are Inevitable

1. Randy Alcorn, *If God Is Good* (Colorado Springs: Multnomah, 2009), 17.

2. *Webster's New Riverside Dictionary*, rev. ed., s.v. "overwhelmed."

3. Oswald Chambers, *My Utmost for His Highest* (Grand Rapids: Discovery House Publishers, 1992), November 13.

4. *Webster's New Riverside Dictionary*, s.v. "surrender."

5. Chambers, *My Utmost for His Highest*, June 27.

### Chapter 3: The Forgotten Promise

1. Kari West, *Dare to Trust, Dare to Hope Again* (Colorado Springs: David C. Cook, 2001), 117.

2. Sarah Young, *Jesus Calling* (Nashville: Thomas Nelson, 2004), 380.

3. Debbie Alsdorf, *He Is My Freedom* (Colorado Springs: David C. Cook, 2000), 20.

4. Ibid., 21.

### Chapter 4: God Holds You Together

1. Oswald Chambers, *My Utmost for His Highest* (Grand Rapids: Discovery House Publishers, 1992), January 1.

2. *Webster's New Riverside Dictionary*, rev. ed., s.v. "identity."

### Chapter 5: God Is Always at Work

1. Oswald Chambers, *My Utmost for His Highest* (Grand Rapids: Discovery House Publishers, 1992), January 22.

### Chapter 6: Suffering Is a Part of Life

1. Shauna Niequist, *Bittersweet* (Grand Rapids: Zondervan, 2010), 17.

2. Kari West, *Dare to Trust, Dare to Hope Again* (Colorado Springs: David C. Cook, 2001), 27–28.

### Chapter 7: Develop a New View of Suffering

1. Oswald Chambers, *My Utmost for His Highest* (Grand Rapids: Discovery House Publishers, 1992), September 4.

### Chapter 8: There Is a Plan, Even When It Looks like There Isn't

1. Bob Cull, *Some Things I Have Learned about God from the Life of Joseph* (Kelseyville, CA: Earthen Vessel Productions, 1996), 4.

### Chapter 10: God Will Provide for Your Needs

1. Joyce Meyer, *Beauty for Ashes* (Tulsa: Harrison House, 1994), 153.

2. Richard Foster, *Celebration of Discipline*, 3rd ed. (New York: Harper Collins, 1998), 11, 21.

### Chapter 11: Keep Your Spiritual Focus

1. Oswald Chambers, *My Utmost for His Highest* (Grand Rapids: Discovery House Publishers, 1992), June 18.

2. Richard Foster, *Celebration of Discipline*, 3rd ed. (New York: Harper Collins, 1998), 38.

### Chapter 13: Live with Courage

1. Kari West, *Dare to Trust, Dare to Hope Again* (Colorado Springs: David C. Cook, 2001), 13.

### Chapter 14: Consider Others

1. Oswald Chambers, *My Utmost for His Highest* (Grand Rapids: Discovery House Publishers, 1992), 72.
2. Kari West, *Dare to Trust, Dare to Hope Again* (Colorado Springs: David C. Cook, 2001), 222.

### Chapter 17: Do Everything without Complaining

1. *Webster's New Riverside Dictionary*, rev. ed., s.v. "resolve."
2. Oswald Chambers, *My Utmost for His Highest* (Grand Rapids: Discovery House Publishers, 1992), June 28.

### Chapter 18: Rejoice in the Lord

1. Oswald Chambers, *My Utmost for His Highest* (Grand Rapids: Discovery House Publishers, 1992), January 27.

### Chapter 19: Put Your Confidence in God

1. Oswald Chambers, *My Utmost for His Highest* (Grand Rapids: Discovery House Publishers, 1992), May 2.

### Chapter 20: Forgive Others, Forgive Yourself, and Receive God's Forgiveness

1. Sandra D. Wilson, *Hurt People, Hurt People* (Grand Rapids: Discovery House Publishers, 2001).

### Chapter 21: Watch Your Perspective

1. Oswald Chambers, *My Utmost for His Highest* (Grand Rapids: Discovery House Publishers, 1992), November 1.
2. Tommy Newberry, *The 4:8 Principle* (Carol Stream, IL: Tyndale, 2007), 129–30.

### Chapter 23: Look for the Good and Practice Dwelling There

1. Tommy Newberry, *The 4:8 Principle* (Carol Stream, IL: Tyndale, 2007), 72.

### Appendix B

1. Jim George, *The Bare Bones Bible Handbook* (Eugene, OR: Harvest House, 2006), 303.

2. Outline adapted from Avon Malone, *Press to the Prize* (Nashville: Twentieth-Century Christian Publishers, 1991), 17.

3. Oswald Chambers, *My Utmost for His Highest* (Grand Rapids: Discovery House Publishers, 1992), January 1.

4. Rom. 1:1; 1 Cor. 1:1; 2 Cor. 1:1; Gal. 1:1; Eph. 1:1; 1 Tim. 1:1; 2 Tim. 1:1; Titus 1:1.

5. Malone, *Press to the Prize*, 22.

6. Chambers, *My Utmost for His Highest*, January 1.

7. Ibid.

8. Ibid., June 15.

9. Ibid., May 8.

**Debbie Alsdorf** is the author of *Deeper* and *A Different Kind of Wild*. As the founder of Design4Living Ministries, she seeks to encourage women to Live Up! in the truth of God's Word. Since 1997 she has been the director of women's ministries at Cornerstone Fellowship, where she and her team lead a vibrant women's ministry. Debbie is a biblical lay counselor and a member of the American Association of Christian Counselors. She lives in Northern California.

# Stop Striving for Perfection and Start Living for Real

"Debbie beautifully teaches truth that changes a woman forever."—**Jennifer Rothschild**, author, *Lessons I Learned in the Dark* and *Self.Talk, Soul Talk*

**Revell**
a division of Baker Publishing Group
www.RevellBooks.com

Available wherever books are sold.

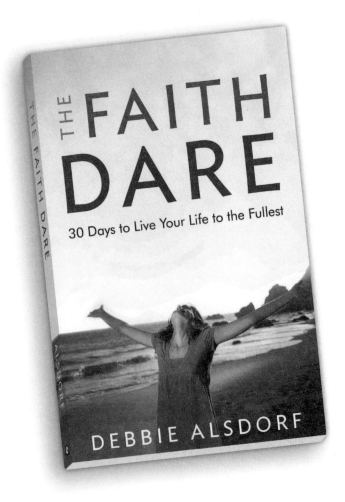

"If you're stuck in a rut in your personal Bible study . . . or you long for God to use you in fresh new ways . . . or you and your small group are tired of pat answers . . . this book is for you!"

—SUSAN ALEXANDER YATES, author of
*A House Full of Friends* and *And Then I Had Kids*

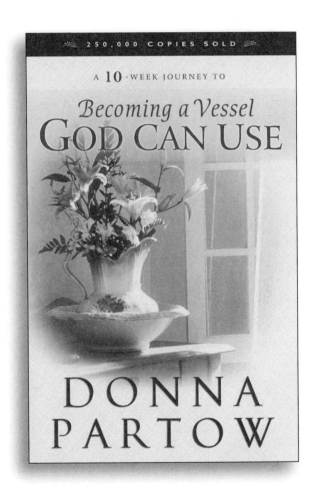

You *can* become the woman God wants you to be. Let this powerful guide renew your energy and determination.

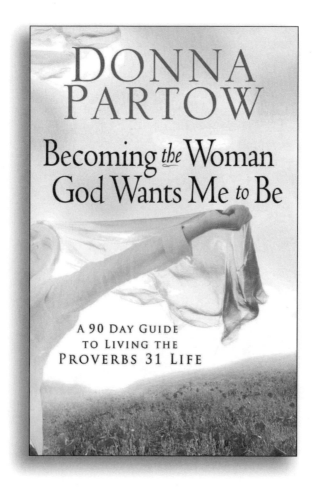

# "Donna's plan will renew you from the inside out— spirit, soul, and body!"

—Danna Demetre, author of *Scale Down*

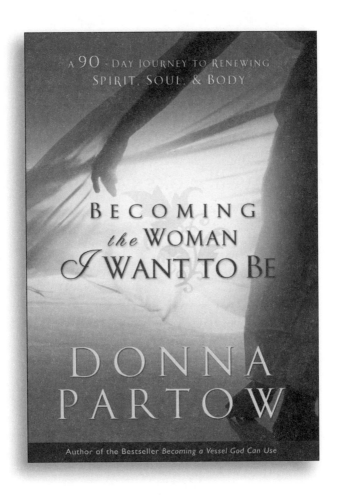